Horizon

NOVEMBER, 1962 · VOLUME V, NUMBER 2

HORIZON
A Magazine of the Arts

NOVEMBER, 1962 · VOLUME V, NUMBER 2

PUBLISHER
James Parton

EDITORIAL DIRECTOR
Joseph J. Thorndike, Jr.

EDITOR
William Harlan Hale

MANAGING EDITOR
Eric Larrabee

ASSOCIATE EDITOR
Ralph Backlund

ASSISTANT EDITORS
Ada Pesin
Jane Wilson
Albert Bermel

CONTRIBUTING EDITOR
Margery Darrell

EDITORIAL ASSISTANTS
Shirley Abbott, Caroline Backlund
Wendy Buehr

COPY EDITOR
Mary Ann Pfeiffer
Assistants: Joan Rehe, Ruth H. Wolfe

ART DIRECTOR
Irwin Glusker
Associate Art Director: Elton Robinson

ADVISORY BOARD
Gilbert Highet, *Chairman*
Frederick Burkhardt   Oliver Jensen
Marshall B. Davidson   Jotham Johnson
Richard M. Ketchum   John Walker

EUROPEAN CONSULTING EDITOR
J. H. Plumb
Christ's College, Cambridge

EUROPEAN BUREAU
Gertrudis Feliu, *Chief*
11 rue du Buloi, Paris

HORIZON is published every two months by American Heritage Publishing Co., Inc. Executive and editorial offices: 551 Fifth Ave., New York 17, N.Y. HORIZON welcomes contributions but can assume no responsibility for unsolicited material.

All correspondence about subscriptions should be addressed to: HORIZON Subscription Office, 379 West Center St., Marion, Ohio.

Single Copies: $4.50
Annual Subscriptions: $21.00 in the U.S. & Can.
$22.00 elsewhere

An annual index is published every September, priced at $1. HORIZON is also indexed in the *Readers Guide to Periodical Literature.*

Title registered U.S. Patent Office

Second-class postage paid at New York, N.Y., and at additional mailing offices.

COVER: This portrait of Saint Jerome is from an especially handsome manuscript copy of his translation of Didymus Alexandrinus's *De Spiritu Sancto.* The book was made in Italy for King Matthias Corvinus of Hungary, whose library in its time rivaled that of the Vatican. After his death in 1490 the great collection began to break up, and in 1541 the bulk of it was seized by the Turks. Since then, Corvinus books have been much sought after, but only two hundred forty-four can be accounted for. Among them is the *De Spiritu Sancto,* which is now in the Pierpont Morgan Library. An article on the ways in which books have managed to survive the ravages of history begins on page 74.

FRONTISPIECE: "The God of Wealth in His Civil Aspect" once belonged, appropriately, to the late John D. Rockefeller, Jr., who bequeathed it to the Metropolitan Museum of Art in 1960. Along with a companion piece of fiercer mien, "The God of Wealth in His Military Aspect," it is an outstanding example of Chinese porcelain of the K'ang Hsi period (1662–1722). The 23-inch-high figure is in five colors of enamel, the throne and crown are gilded silver, and the holes are for inserting a beard of human hair.

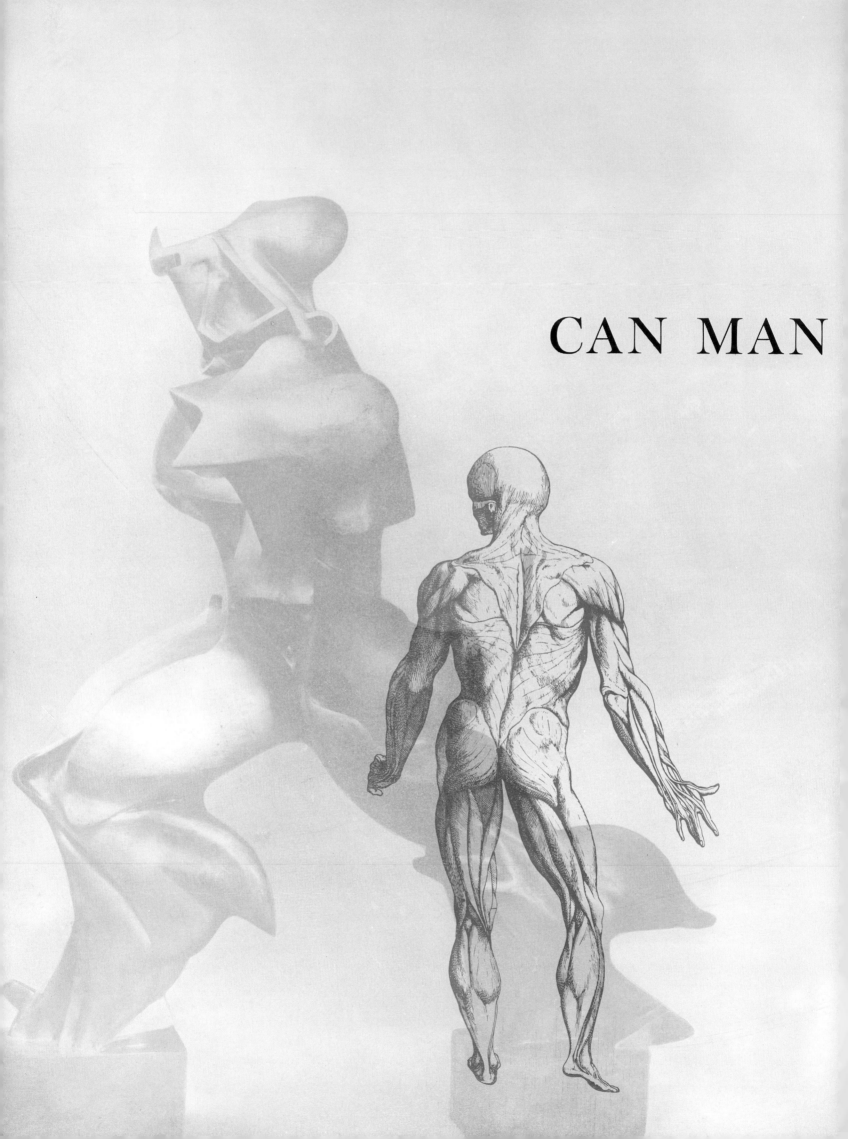

CAN MAN

KEEP UP WITH HISTORY?

The large cities of the modern world remind one of beehives and of ant hills. Each individual person in them has a specialized function and returns to rest at a particular place as if he were but one among so many other interchangeable units in an immense colony. As human societies become larger, older, and more dependent on technology, the colonial organization becomes more intricate and more inflexible. The formal resemblance between human institutions and the colonies of social insects is indeed so striking as to make one fear that modern man is doomed to become a specialized worker or soldier in a stereotyped social machine. Fortunately, the formal resemblances are misleading, because human societies differ in a fundamental way both in origin and in structure from all known insect colonies. Whereas each of the latter represents a gigantic single family, human societies represent groupings of many families. Whatever their degree of specialization, all the members of a given insect colony are like so many brothers and sisters from the same parents. The members of human groups are bound by social ties, but they differ in genetic make-up.

The great genetic diversity of human beings in most parts of the world provides an immense range of potentialities for evolutionary development. Furthermore, evolution in man is now primarily of a psychosocial nature, and the great density of human populations increases enormously the rate of change by facilitating contacts and cross-fertilization of ideas. But, while it is certain that human societies will continue to evolve, the unsolved problem is to determine the direction in which they will or should evolve.

In many ways, the formulation of adequate goals for social development is now far more difficult than it was during earlier phases of civilization. In the past the production of food, shelter, and clothing, the limitation of physical effort, the control of all forms of suffering, constituted well-defined objectives which could be reached by technological improvements. The pursuit of knowledge for its own sake was also simpler. Scholars worked individually on questions that interested them. Receiving little recognition or help from the community, they had much intellectual freedom in the selection of their field of endeavor. The situation is now different because the elementary problems of survival have been solved, and also because the scientist has become a paid servant of the state. As a result, the question of what to do next, which used to concern chiefly the individual, now must be considered by the social group.

We have enormous resources, and powerful means of action. The difficulty is to choose what is most worth doing among all the things that can and should be done. Should we increase further the comfort and ease of life; abolish more completely all forms of suffering and tedious work; strive for deeper knowledge and understanding of the universe or greater aesthetic appreciation; achieve more intimate communion with the cosmos; try to bring about a true brotherhood among men? All these purposes, and many others, are worthy of human effort, but they cannot all be pursued simultaneously with equal vigor. There will have to be choices, based on judgments of value.

The nearer man comes to complete mastery of the physical world, the more urgent it is for him to imagine further worthwhile goals. The alternative is spiritual stagnation, failure to find outlets for human energies and talents, and in the end, boredom and unhappiness. It is of some interest in this regard that sociological studies are beginning to detect evidence of minor but significant changes in the goals of the American society. Recent surveys have shown, for example, that many American males are becoming less concerned with the economic well-being of their dependents and more likely to emphasize, instead, problems of interpersonal relationships, such as fulfilling the manly role at home, guiding the family, spend-

By RENE DUBOS

ing more time with the children, etc. President Kennedy's adviser W. W. Rostow went as far as to suggest, in his book *The Stages of Economic Growth,* that the trend toward larger families in the United States derives in part from a desire to recapture some aspects of the "strenuous life," now that the desire for material conveniences has been almost satiated.

The possibility in the Western world to satisfy most of the physical needs essential for pleasant living signifies that mankind is about to reach one of its evolutionary peaks. Clearly, however, evolutionary trends other than the search for comfort began long ago. Artistic expression dates at least from the Paleolithic era—twenty thousand years ago—and yet it does not correspond to any material necessity. The pursuit of pure knowledge is also very ancient; theoretical science was studied even when it had no apparent practical applications, and there would still be many theoretical scientists today even if they were no longer needed for technological development.

It is certain, therefore, that one can conceive of many possible evolutionary directions for human societies. In final analysis, these directions will be determined by judgments of value as to what makes life worth living. But equally important is the fact that the growth of all forms of knowledge will certainly suggest new goals and values of which we are not yet aware. To take one example, the fact that the future is open and unpredictable has large medical and educational implications. As we shall see, it makes adaptability the key concept in the care of the body and the cultivation of the mind.

According to encyclopedias, health is a condition free of disease and of discomfort in which the body and the mind are normal and function well. In practice, however, the word health cannot be defined in such abstract terms because it refers to very different states, depending upon the environmental conditions as well as the professional requirements and the aspirations of each particular person. For example, to be healthy means something very different for a Chinese farmer, an American businessman, the pilot of a supersonic plane, a Benedictine nun, or a fashion model in Paris.

The traditional role of medicine and of public health has been to prevent or correct, as far as it is possible, the accidents and malfunctions of the body and of the mind that interfere with human activities, and that shorten life or render it less pleasant. Experience has shown, however, that as one social disease is rooted out, another one springs up to take its place, and there are good reasons to believe that this will continue to plague mankind as long as the conditions of life will continue to change. In this respect physicians and public-health officers are like gardeners and farmers who have to fight weeds and pests. Their work is never finished, and they must continuously adapt their techniques to new problems.

Who could have dreamed a generation ago that overnutrition and hypervitaminosis would become common forms of nutritional disease in the Western world; that the cigarette, automobile exhausts, other air pollutants, and ionizing radiation would be held responsible for the increase in certain types of cancer; that the introduction of detergents and various synthetics would increase the incidence of allergies; that advances in the use of drugs and other therapeutic procedures would create a new pattern of infections; that alcoholics and patients with various forms of chemically induced disease would occupy such a large number of beds in the modern hospital; that an eminent British epidemiologist could refer to some maladies of our times as "pathologies of inactivity" and as "occupational hazards of sedentary and light work"? Since we can take it for granted that everything will continue to change, endlessly, ideal health will always remain an ever-receding mirage. Perfect harmony between man and his environment would have existed only if there had been a time when the world was stable and ideally suited to human needs. But the Golden Age is only a legend, and it will not come to pass in a utopian future.

Christopher Columbus expressed admiration, in the account of his travels, for the beautiful physical state of the natives he had found in the West Indies. Captain Cook, Bougainville, and other navigators who discovered the Pacific islands also marveled at the state of health of Polynesians at that time; and similar reports came from travelers who first saw the American Indians in the Great Plains and in the Rio Grande Valley. Ever since, the experience of explorers has been that most primitive people living in isolated communities are vigorous and happy as long as they retain their ancestral ways of life, whereas physical decadence sets in within one generation after they come into contact with white men. On the basis of these facts it seems fair to state that the health of primitive people, like that of animals in the wild state, depends upon some sort of equilibrium with their environment, and that it breaks down when the conditions of their existence suddenly change. What is true of primitive people also applies to civilized man. The general statement can be made that health depends upon fitness to the environment; it involves a state of adaptiveness.

New diseases appeared among the Polynesians, the American Indians, and the Eskimos after they came into contact with Western civilization because changed circumstances created new adaptive demands for which these people were not prepared. Thus the state of adaptiveness is only one of the components of health; another is the physiological power to react rapidly and effectively to the difficult and unforeseeable situations which occur inevitably whenever the social equilibrium is disturbed. The need for adaptability is especially critical in dynamic societies where living conditions are in a constant state of flux.

An increasing rate of change is inevitable: Can man now bend it to his advantage?

The more complete the human freedom, the more open the future, the greater the likelihood that new stresses will appear —organic and psychic—because man himself continuously changes his environment through technology, and because he endlessly moves into new conditions during his restless search for adventure. The state of adaptiveness prevailing in ancient agrarian societies proved almost useless under the conditions created by the nineteenth-century Industrial Revolution. The Western world has now reached an acceptable state of adaptiveness—social, emotional, and physical—to the type of industrial and urban life that emerged during the nineteenth century, but this is only a transitory state. New problems are being created at present by the countless and profound changes resulting from the second Industrial Revolution, and men will have to develop a new adaptive state in order to function effectively in the Automation Age.

Changeability is more and more the dominant factor in human life. In fact one of the few unchangeable aspects of the human condition is that man must struggle to adapt himself to the ever-changing environment. There is nothing tragic in this situation nor is it peculiar to man. It is the fate of all living things, and it is indeed the law and the very essence of life. However, granted the universality of change, it must be recognized that the problems of adaptation are presently taking a somewhat different aspect for the human race.

In the past the changes in the conditions of life were generally slow, and it took several generations before they could affect all parts of the world and all social classes. This slow tempo made it possible for the full spectrum of adaptive forces to come into play. The physiological and even the physical characteristics of the body became progressively altered in order to meet the new conditions, as did the social customs and the mental reactions. In contrast, technology now upsets the conditions of life so fast and its effects become so widespread all over the world that the biological and social processes of adaptation cannot occur rapidly enough to keep pace. It is becoming more and more difficult for the social body to achieve equilibrium with the new forces that it sets in motion and to which it is therefore not adapted. Biologically and socially, the experience of the father has become almost useless for the son.

For man, adaptation involves his expectations—both his dreams and his fears. Furthermore, each person is a member of the human brotherhood, and the concept of health therefore implies a large component of social responsibility. To be completely successful, adaptation should in consequence contribute to the performance and the growth of the social group as a whole. It is essential to remember in this regard that the medical consequences of many of our present social activities will become manifest only in the years to come. Who can foretell the distant consequences of the fact that modern man no longer experiences the inclemencies of the weather, need not engage in physical exertion, can use drugs to alleviate almost any form of pain, and increasingly depends on tranquilizers and stimulants to live through the day? These achievements have, of course, made life easier and often more pleasant, but they may bring about an atrophy of the adaptive mechanisms which continue to be essential for the maintenance of health.

The usual definitions of health are therefore incomplete, because they consider the problem from an egotistic and static point of view. These definitions are formulated only in terms of the individual person, whereas they should consider also the collectivity. They are concerned with the present instead of emphasizing the future. They regard health as a state. But the most important and interesting aspect of health is not its state but its potentiality. Just as wars are won, not with the weapons available at the beginning of the conflict, but with the new ones built out of potential resources as they are needed, similarly health is the expression of the extent to which the individual and the social body maintain in readiness the resources required to meet the exigencies of the future.

We are gaining the power to control our own genetic inheritance. But to what ends?

The concept of health outlined in the preceding paragraphs implies, of course, the freedom to choose and the possibility for man to will his future, within the limits imposed by natural forces. To believe in free will is, of course, a matter of faith, but what is certain is that man has a large reserve of adaptive potentialities from which to draw, if he has freedom to choose. Among mammalians, man is distinguished by a lack of biological specialization. This has enabled him to live under a wide range of climatic conditions, to eat many kinds of foods, and to engage in countless occupations. His future will measure up to his past only if he can retain the ability, the desire, and the will to carry on his adaptive evolution and thus meet successfully the new trials that he will certainly have to face. Greater knowledge of the range of adaptive potentialities in the human species, and the development of techniques for strengthening them, thus constitutes the scientific basis for the health of the future.

Under natural circumstances, plant and animal populations become adapted to their environment through the selective reproduction of the biologically successful mutant forms. In man, also, natural selection has operated in the past and continues to operate at the present time. There is no doubt that profound changes can occur in the genetic endowment of man—as illustrated by the differences in physical and physiological characteristics between populations living in the Arctic and those adapted to the tropics. To a large extent the ability to master intellectual and behavioral problems is also an innate endowment. It is built into the genetic apparatus just as is resistance to physical and mental stresses. The human child begins to smile at three months of age, independently of any training or fondling; the eagerness to play and to explore also seems to be genetically inherited, as well as are other patterns of intelligence and of response to the environment.

Hereditary changes in man have resulted so far from undirected processes, blind selective forces tending to favor the survival of the persons best fitted to a given environment. A few geneticists believe, however, that the time has now come to control scientifically the evolutionary changes, in order to prevent the degenerative effects of civilization on the human stock. Whereas mutation rates are increasing, our ways of life are interfering with the elimination of undesirable genes; natural selection is more and more embarrassed by social and medical practices. True enough, the genetic processes of degeneration are so slow that one is tempted to shrug off their effects, because most of them take hundreds of years to become evident. As in the case of erosion, they come to be accepted as a part of the natural order. Social scientists and men of affairs are no more interested in such remote problems than is the general public. The fact is, however, that the most destructive, as well as the most creative, operations of the living world have been of a creeping, extended character. In the long run they are probably the most influential determinants of the future of the human race.

In view of these facts it would seem logical to take advantage of modern biological knowledge and attempt some measure of control over the hereditary endowment of man. The celebrated American geneticist Hermann J. Muller has recently made concrete proposals to this effect. What Professor Muller suggests is simply the widespread practice of artificial insemination, using for this purpose preserved sperm obtained from human males whose life record is well known. According to him, this policy of positive eugenics would facilitate the spread through the general population of a number of desirable genetic characters, including physical and intellectual endowment.

Professor Muller's program of positive eugenics has stirred up passionate controversies, and there is as yet no indication that it will be applied on any significant scale. Objections to it come from two very different angles. First is the fact that genetic science is not yet sufficiently developed to permit prediction of what will happen if steps are taken to control human evolution. Many geneticists take, in this regard, a position almost completely opposite to that of Professor Muller; they claim that far from trying to channel genetic make-up in certain directions, we should maintain as much genetic diversity as possible. It is important, according to Professor P. B. Medawar, to "maintain a population versatile enough to cope with hazards that change from time to time and from place to place. A case can be made for saying that a genetical system that attaches great weight to genetic diversity is part of our heritage, and part of the heritage of most other free, living, and outbreeding organisms." Instead of trying to tailor man to a future which is at best dimly visualized, it is probably wiser at this stage to develop a culture fitted to man's needs.

The other fundamental objection to positive eugenics is that no one really knows what characteristics to breed in order to improve the human stock. Everyone agrees, of course, that it would be desirable to eliminate certain obviously objectionable traits, such as gross physical and mental defects—though even this limited program poses problems of judgment and execution far more complex than is usually realized. But the selection of positive qualities raises questions of a much more subtle nature.

Many qualities we most prize now may not be the ones the future will demand in us

It is relatively easy to formulate a genetic program aimed at producing larger pigs, faster horses, better hunting dogs, or more friendly cats. But what is the ideal for human societies? The cave man, for all his strength and resourcefulness, would not get along well in a modern city. On the other hand, our present way of life may soon be antiquated, and future life may demand a kind of endurance undreamed of at the present time. For all we know, resistance to radiation, to noise, to intense light, to the monotony of continuous stimuli, and to the eternal repetition of boring activities may become essential for biological success in future civilizations. Who knows, furthermore, whether mankind is better served by the gentleness of Saint Francis of Assisi and Fra Angelico or by the dynamism of the Industrial Revolution and modern art? Is the higher type of society one that prizes, above all, individual development or one that regards devotion to the common welfare as the highest standard of morality? Is it at all desirable to reproduce on a large scale a trait the appeal of which is perhaps its uniqueness? How many Beethovens would it take to make his genius commonplace? Furthermore, would a human being endowed with Beethoven's genes have the kind of musical genius enabling him to express the moods of the Automation Age?

The fundamental difficulty in formulating a program for the genetic improvement of man is that we do not know what we are nor where we are, what we want to become nor where we want to go. In fact mankind has not yet developed the skill to think effectively about these problems. To a large extent we still hold to a static and mechanical view of the universe and of life. The discussions about evolutionary development rarely encompass a continuously emergent novelty, an open future, not predictable from what is known. Yet this is probably the most profound meaning of the evolutionary concept—a view of life as a continuous act of creation, in which man has become the most important actor.

There is, however, good reason for believing that without resorting to genetic manipulation man can train himself to be more effective and more creative. Every person has in reserve a wide range of potentialities—both physical and mental—which remain unexpressed. As is well known, anyone can, with a little systematic effort, become better at almost any task and more resistant to almost any kind of stress. Because the dominant trend in our civilization has been to control the environment, little has been learned of the extent to which it is possible to modify, by systematic and continued effort, the human machine and the human mind. Nevertheless, there are a number of isolated facts that point to large possibilities in this direction.

Experiments with laboratory animals have shown that it is possible by adequate stimulation to tune up the organism for more rapid and more efficient responses to the environment, such as, release of certain hormones, development of adaptive mechanisms, production of antibodies. Exposure to various forms of stimuli and stresses during the very early stages of development renders the animals sturdier, emotionally more stable, and more efficient at learning tasks. Particularly striking is the fact that the ability to learn is conditioned by early exposure to the proper kind of stimuli. This has been shown by measuring the ability of rats to perform in a maze and observing the eagerness with which they explore an unknown environment. The intelligence and intellectual curiosity of rats handled frequently during the first twenty days of life is greater than that of animals which have not been stimulated.

Baby chimpanzees kept in the dark for a few months after birth later on have greater difficulty than ordinary animals in recognizing colors and shapes, even though their eyesight is completely normal. A similar situation is observed in human beings who lacked pattern vision in childhood. Even though the eye defect can be corrected by removing an opaque lens or transplanting a clear cornea, these persons experience great difficulty in learning to distinguish a square from a circle.

Both body and soul will have to be steeled against new kinds of stress and strain

As already mentioned, little is known of the extent of human potentialities, because the trend of civilization has been to control and modify the external environment for the sake of comfort, the ideal goal being total elimination of effort and suffering. We do little, if anything, to train the body and soul to resist strains and stresses; but we devote an enormous amount of skill and foresight to conditioning our dwellings against heat and cold, avoiding contact with germs, making food available at all hours of the day, multiplying labor-saving devices, dulling even the slightest pain with drugs, and minimizing the effort of learning. The enormous success of these practices in making life more pleasant and more effective has, unfortunately, led to the neglect of another approach for dealing with the external world, namely, the cultivation of the resources in human nature that make man potentially adaptable to a wide range of living conditions.

There is at present little scientific knowledge concerning the mechanisms involved in adaptation, and this ignorance makes it difficult to formulate the problem rationally. Nevertheless there is reason to believe that science can develop techniques conducive to greater adaptability and yet compatible with the values of civilized life. This belief is based on the fact that nature itself is the great healer. There exist in the body many natural systems of defense which protect the various organs and functions against most forms of injury—whether these originate from nature or from technological civilization. If man can really learn to cultivate and enhance his defense mechanisms, he will be better able to function pleasantly and effectively in the new world he is creating. Furthermore, development of these potentialities may soon become essential, be-

cause it is futile to hope that the environment can be controlled sufficiently to assure passive health and happiness. More and more, adaptation will be an active process demanding continuous efforts.

Many of the stresses that man encounters in the modern world affect the mind first and the body only secondarily. For this reason adaptive mechanisms having their seat in the mind are as important as those affecting the body machine. Man can learn by experience to resist suffering, to make intellectual efforts, to overcome impatience, to manifest activity. A society that depends on sedatives or stimulants to continue functioning cannot achieve the state of resilience necessary for survival, let alone for growth.

The need to regard adaptation as a creative process involving continuous effort applies also to the process of learning. In a world where everything changes rapidly, the practical facts learned in school soon become obsolete. The techniques and equipment that are the most up-to-date expression of knowledge during the school years are usually outmoded by the time the student begins to function in adult life. The only knowledge of permanent value is theoretical knowledge; and the broader it is, the greater the chances that it will prove useful in practice, because it will be applicable to a wide range of conditions. The persons most likely to become creative and to act as leaders are not those who enter life with the largest amount of detailed, specialized information, but rather those who have enough theoretical knowledge, critical judgment, and discipline of learning to adapt rapidly to the new situations and problems which constantly arise in the modern world.

These qualifications are not acquired without effort, and may even demand painful effort. In fact, it may well be dangerous to make learning passive and effortless, because one of the most important aspects of education should be to instill the willingness to engage in difficult intellectual work. Like health, learning cannot be acquired passively. It is an active process, and the measure of its success is the extent to which it enables the individual to adapt to the unpredictable circumstances of life and thereby to meet them successfully.

The fact that adaptation will increasingly demand conscious efforts need not imply a tragic view of life. The necessity to respond vigorously to the environment and the efforts involved in mastering oneself, as well as in learning, are precisely the elements that give structure and meaning to life. For, in final analysis, the potentialities of human beings are realized only by meeting challenges in a creative spirit. History teaches that man without effort is sure to deteriorate; man cannot progress without effort, and man cannot be happy without it.

A leading bacteriologist and member of the Rockefeller Institute for Medical Research, René Dubos has also written widely concerning science in its relation to general culture—as in his essay "The Dream of Reason" in the July, 1961, HORIZON. The present essay will appear in his forthcoming The Torch of Life, *published by Pocket Books.*

Calder en Campagne

In his summer home in France, the master of the mobile paints and putters amid

The carnival disorder of Alexander Calder's main studio (opposite), a converted barn next to his house, reflects the many directions his work is taking. The burst of fireworks against the wall behind his head (below) is a recent experiment in gouache.

Photographs by HANS NAMUTH

the airy, restless metal-and-wire sculptures that are his unique artistic invention

By JEAN DAVIDSON

The author, whose father was the sculptor Jo Davidson, is the son-in-law of his subject, and consequently writes from close acquaintance.

For those who meet him for the first time, either in his home at Roxbury, Connecticut, or in Saché, France, where he spends the summer, Alexander Calder is a puzzling personality. A big, two-hundred-twenty-pound man, he will be wearing either a red or dark blue flannel shirt and a pair of dungarees, with a large leather belt fastened by a hammered buckle of his own making. He is a bit untidy, rather than sloppy, always negligently at ease. His forehead is broad, his hair snow white. Though he may resemble someone who has just come off a successful farm or from a traveling show, there is an assurance, a spontaneity, a placid weight in the gaze, that contradicts his costume. His hands may tremble a bit now, but his thoughts never do. On closer scrutiny, Calder resembles not a worker or a farmer but a victorious revolutionary general—which is in fact what he is. Sculpture will never again be quite what it was before him.

One of the few new art forms of the past two thousand years is the mobile, which Calder invented—an arrangement of wire and pieces of metal which turn in space, forming ever-changing patterns and sculptural volumes; an abstraction, in other words, in three dimensions and in motion. In the course of his career Calder has also made portraits in wire, and sturdy motionless metal sculptures that he calls "stabiles"; recently, in addition, he has been painting large, bold compositions in gouache. But Calder is most widely known as the man who makes the mobiles. This past summer, when the largest restrospective show of his work ever held opened at the Tate Gallery in London, the usual museum formula could appropriately have been reversed to read: "Please Touch the Exhibits." The London *Times* complimented Calder on a "playful and joyous exhibition," and reporters noted that the guards were encouraging small boys to push the mobiles, suspended from the high gallery ceiling, into graceful movement. Calder, in whom something of the small boy has always remained, was delighted.

Sandy Calder is an American, with all the coarseness, the strength, the practical and inventive turn of mind, the restless energy and buoyancy of the early pioneers. "His vernacular," writes his biographer, James Johnson Sweeney, "is the vernacular of his age in America—an age in which the frontiers of science, engineering, and mechanics have dominated the popular imagination in the same way that the national frontier dominated it a century ago." But his Yankee flavor is never provincial, his gaiety is always genuine, and his exploration of controlled movement is more advanced than anything recently achieved in Europe.

For Jean-Paul Sartre, often critical of things American, Calder "catches" true live movements and fashions them; "a mobile is a little local fair, an object defined by its movements which do not exist outside of it, a flower that withers as soon as it is stopped, a pure play of movement, just as there are pure plays of light. . . . For each one of his mobiles Calder establishes a general career of movement and then abandons it; it is the time of day, the sunshine, the heat, the wind, which determine each individual dance. Thus the object remains midway between the enslaved statue and a free, natural occurrence. . . . Of the sea, Valéry used to say that it is always beginning over again. One of Calder's objects is like the sea and like it casts a spell; always begun over again, always new. So the imagination is cheered by these pure shapes, their free or guided translations . . . the timid development, endlessly delayed, thwarted, or held together by an Idea."

Alexander Calder was born in Philadelphia on July 22, 1898, into an unexceptionally conventional world of the *beaux-arts*. His father, A. Stirling Calder, was a National Academician and one of the best sculptors of his generation. Calder's mother was a painter, but she decided to devote her time to her husband and their two children, Sandy and his sister Peggy. She had a vigorous, rather masculine streak, and in later years often regretted not having given more of her life to painting. Sandy's grandfather, Alexander Milne Calder, born in Scotland, was also a sculptor. His statue of William Penn stands today atop the Philadelphia City Hall. He had won his first national recognition with an equestrian statue of General Meade.

Eleven Red, 1960

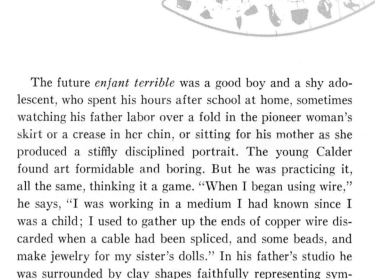

Blue Tongued Fish, 1957

The future *enfant terrible* was a good boy and a shy adolescent, who spent his hours after school at home, sometimes watching his father labor over a fold in the pioneer woman's skirt or a crease in her chin, or sitting for his mother as she produced a stiffly disciplined portrait. The young Calder found art formidable and boring. But he was practicing it, all the same, thinking it a game. "When I began using wire," he says, "I was working in a medium I had known since I was a child; I used to gather up the ends of copper wire discarded when a cable had been spliced, and some beads, and make jewelry for my sister's dolls." In his father's studio he was surrounded by clay shapes faithfully representing symmetry and order; a monumental sculpture of Saint Denis—carrying his head in his arms—was the farthest his father ever strayed from literal-minded realism. Many years later, the son was to formulate a law that his father's art had consistently violated: "Disparity in form, color, size, weight, motion, is what makes a composition. . . . It is the apparent accident to regularity which the artist actually controls by which he makes or mars a work."

In spite of his lively childhood drawings, and a knack with wire and tin, Sandy turned his back on art after he completed high school, and enrolled instead in the Stevens Institute of Technology. The record shows that he graduated a full engineer with splendid marks in descriptive geometry—that art of transcribing projected planes to a flat sheet of paper, with all the multitudinous lines of their intersections.

After that Calder did a bit of everything. He worked in a logging camp in the state of Washington. He looked at the landscape: mountains on one side, lakes on the other. To make a complete picture of it he painted two landscapes from opposite angles, then joined them end to end in order to re-create on flat canvas his circular field of vision. In the camp he had a chance to indulge for the first time some of the simplicity and vigorousness of his nature. "At lunch time," he says, "the bosses supplied vast quantities of food, pancakes and bacon galore, because this robbed the most aggressive of the chance to talk the others into a scrap." He disliked physical violence, as he had from earliest days. "When I was a kid, I

had a lot of toys, but I was never quite satisfied with them. I always improved and enlarged the array with wire contrivances, copper, and other materials. In California I had a pal: we'd build armor and weapons out of tin and boxwood. He was Sir Lancelot and I was Sir Tristram. We expected to indulge in a friendly fight, but he was much nimbler and once he gave me a blow with the flat of his wooden sword on my behind. I dropped out of the arena forever."

From the logging camp he went East and then to sea, working his way during the summer of 1922 in a freighter through the Panama Canal back to California, where he and his parents had been living for some years. Still, it was not really adventure to scrape fuel burners in an overheated engine room. Sandy retired to the repair shop in his off hours and hammered out a special scraper. The new tool worked wonders, and his mates in the engine room all wanted one, so he went on hammering. But the food was poor, and he was afflicted with boils on his legs. He cut off his trousers at knee length to avoid friction; now splashes of fuel oil only increased his misery. The next solution was to sew kneepads to the abbreviated trouser legs, and from then on he was known as the Kneepad Boy. The problem of the burners and of his knees neatly solved, there was still that of the stifling heat. So Calder went up on the bridge and rigged a canvas scoop in front of the air shaft. The men not on duty drenched it from time to time with buckets of sea water. The result was a fresh breeze into the hold.

Between the air conditioning and the special scrapers, Calder was the first efficiency and comfort engineer this steamship line had ever known. If the voyage had lasted longer, oven doors would soon have been opened and closed at a distance by metal rods, worked by smiling men lounging in improvised easy chairs in the shade of varicolored canvas awnings. But, of course, the threat of a working journey with the appearance of a pleasure cruise was too much for the captain, who promptly fired Calder as soon as the boat docked in California. Calder retained ever after a wholly unconnected visual impression of this voyage: a red sun chasing the white ball of the moon across the Pacific.

One odd job followed another. After a week in a foundry

MOBILES AND STABILE COURTESY PERLS GALLERY, N.Y.

White Flower, Red Flower, c. 1950

At the heart of Calder's compound in France is a sturdy 15th-century stone farmhouse; in the courtyard is one of his outdoor works

department of an automotive firm, Calder proposed to the director several simple improvements in design and manufacturing methods. He was fired on the spot. Later he found himself working as an assessor for an insurance company. The director made the rounds one day asking if everything was O.K. Calder pointed to a naked light bulb overhead. "This thing hurts my eyes."

"I don't give a damn about your eyes!"

"This guy didn't give a damn about my eyes," says Calder, "so I took my coat and left."

These unsatisfactory experiences were probably what persuaded him to seek solace in the old family pursuit. In the fall of 1923 he enrolled in the New York Art Students League. Here he drew and made a few wire objects; and one of them —the first, his famous wire rooster—he installed as a part of a sundial on the window ledge of his furnished room. One of his teachers was Guy Pène duBois, a painter of pretty women and springy deer bounding through sunlit country scenes. DuBois did these oils so nicely, and with such earnestness, that Sandy liked him and did not care whether the more sophisticated pupils thought DuBois's paintings looked like expensive candy-box tops. Yet there is no trace of his teacher in Calder's early drawings; quite the contrary, for they were drawn to be published in the *National Police Gazette*—gym scenes, boxing matches, circuses. "The drawings are not distinguished," says James Johnson Sweeney. "Throughout the series, however, we already see hints of the humor and observation that mark his mature work. This is especially true of the captions." Thus we find, in the *Police Gazette* of May 23, 1925, over Calder's forceful signature, a drawing of a tightrope walker with the caption "Direct by wire."

In 1926 he left the *Police Gazette* and went to Paris. "The first year I was there," he says, "I met a Serb who claimed he was a toy salesman and told me I could earn a good living by inventing mechanical toys. As I did not have too many nickels, this caught my interest. I started right away." (To this day "right away" and "I can't wait" remain pet Calder phrases.) "I used wire as the main material and added all kinds of things—string, leather, cloth, wood. Wood combined with wire—with which I did the heads, tails, and ani-

mals' legs, and also the articulations—was my standard procedure. A friend suggested that I make figures out of wire alone, and this is how I started making what I called wire sculptures. In Montparnasse they soon called me the Wire King. My Serb had disappeared long since, but I remained busy making toys and decided to create a whole circus."

Before long, Calder could be found kneeling in front of a group of guests, seated on the floor or studio couch, presenting his acrobats, tumblers, trained dogs, slack-wire set, lion tamer, and belly dancer; his Charles Rigolot (*"l'homme le plus fort du monde"*); the Sultan of Senegambia, who hurled axes and knives; Don Rodriguez Kolynos, who risked death in a wire-sliding stunt; a trapeze act; and even a chariot race. A spotlight would be thrown on the ring, a bit of carpet unrolled, a phonograph set playing a fanfare, and Calder himself would bark out: *"Mesdames, Messieurs, je vous présente le Cirque Calder."*

One day his friends suggested to the Wire King of Montparnasse that he visit the studio of the Mad Dutchman, Piet Mondrian. This aging genius, tired of painting his rectilinear landscapes, had blocked up most of his windows with plywood and was spending his time listening to jazz records. Confronted by Mondrian's canvases, Calder was stunned by the simple color masses and the black stems linking them together. Afterward, Calder told his friend the surrealist Marcel Duchamp, "I want to make Mondrians that move." Duchamp answered simply: "You will, Sandy, and you will call them mobiles."

Thus in the year 1930, in Paris, was born the Calder we have since come to know, the son of a classical academician who did not understand his son's wire sculpture "because you cannot fondle it"; son, too, of Piet Mondrian, and godson to Marcel Duchamp, who was among the first to understand Calder's importance and significance.

After the visit to Mondrian's studio, Calder set to work with simple wire and aluminum sheet metal to find a means of achieving patterned rhythms of moving shapes within a determined field. In time his love of the spectacular, of colliding contrasts, of Mondrian, of the solar system, his fondness for metal and wire and articulations, began to express themselves; and the unprecedented art forms that resulted began to find their way into museums. *Bayonets Menacing a Flower*—ominous fixed shapes, all painted black, sharply pursuing mobile white petals—was made fifteen years after the visit to Mondrian's studio and represents a long evolution from the first of Calder's mobiles, some of them motor-driven, some mere shapes or volumes dangling at the end of strings. The evolution does not cease, though Calder has sometimes paused while hammering out an element for a new mobile to wonder whether he was becoming ingrown, habit-bound, uninventive. But each time a new creative urge has followed his unrest. In America, during World War II, fearing a shortage of the indispensable aluminum plate, he invented an entire new family of objects, the "Constellations," carved wooden volumes springing from wire stems. In 1958 he filled the showroom of the Galerie Maeght in Paris with huge stainless-steel shapes painted black—with one exception, called *Semaphore*, composed in brilliant colors.

Georges Salles, Director of the Museums of France (whose grandfather designed the Eiffel Tower), wrote in wonderment: "The stabiles shown here are ponderous steel monuments, but their thickness brings out the sensitive quality of their innate lightness. . . . Born in the surcharged atmosphere of the New World, Calder is the storyteller of our age—his machines may not be able to talk, but he grants the power of expression to a metal species of his own—his metallic fauna populate our world with new dinosaurs. . . . Structures sharpen their spikes, display bare blades, cast overhead a harvest of steel. Bolts, flanges, fins, reinforced ribs, jagged steel plates, threaten us. Walk around these monuments, however, bend under their arcs, cast a glance through their openings, and you will [be brought] back to the smiling domain of life. We are with the poet."

Today Calder is accustomed to eulogies. He has erected a huge monument, *Black Spiral*, in front of the UNESCO Building in Paris. He has hung large mobiles in American airports, Idlewild, and Pittsburgh; the Pittsburgh mobile won the Carnegie Prize. "I designed it to dwarf the ornate 1900 staircase of the museum where it was first shown," says Calder. (It did.) For the National Museum in Stockholm he built the biggest motor-driven mobile in the world: the ensemble, made up of three revolving elements, stands thirty feet high. For more than one fair Calder has designed a stunning surprise: the first was his Mercury Fountain for the 1937 Paris Exposition, and it stole the show. He created another surprise, *The Whirling Ear,* in front of the American Pavilion at the Brussels Fair.

Sandy's father liked to contemplate the destiny of man—like many artists of that period, he thought it a part of his responsibiliy. Sandy would much rather sit at a table, well-provided with simple food and red wine, surrounded by his friends. Success has not changed his ways. Despite his care-free attitude, he has retained from his early days a great regard for economy and will save discarded boxes, pieces of string, aluminum scraps, any of which might come in handy someday. His humor is as coarse and direct as his appearance—or as his *Police Gazette* captions. To the journalist who asked him when he knew that a mobile was finished, he replied: "When it's time to eat."

In 1953 Calder began summering in the southern part of France, and in 1954 he moved north to the town of Saché in the château country, into a fifteenth-century stone house in the valley of the Indre near Azay-le-Rideau (I traded it to him myself for four mobiles). Nearby he has a studio in an old barn, and he has since acquired several other buildings in which to store his works and to paint in gouache. This very year, on a nearby hilltop that is one of the most beautiful sites in the valley, he began to build a new studio of his own design which will be the largest he has ever owned. It lies against a little wood, surrounded by vineyards. Recently a friend visited the imposing building, with its eight large arches. "Is this a Roman ruin?" he asked. "Not yet," answered Calder.

For all this modesty, Sandy at sixty-four is conscious of his strength and sometimes only half-jokingly will say: "I'm convinced that this boob Alexander the Great knew nothing about knots. I would have untied the Gordian knot in no time, and without having to throw an axe at it!"

So copious is Calder's output that he has had to convert this studio-stable to storage, while a new workshop is being built up the road

WHEN GOVERNMENT WENT ALL OUT FOR THE ARTS

My dear Mr. President:

I have the honor to submit the following report on the current state of the arts in the United States, particularly as affected during the last fiscal year by programs administered by the Department I have the privilege to head, or by other public agencies which it is my duty as Secretary of Arts and Leisure to co-ordinate.

It is the considered judgment of the Department that the arts, so long neglected from the point of view of public policy, are presently enjoying an unprecedentedly high rate of productivity and consumption, and this is attributable in large part to the spacious program of cultural assistance and development launched by the present Administration. Painting, sculpture, poetry, playwriting, opera and orchestral music, folk balladry and the dance, are all now receiving Federal aid as our first line of cultural defense, and moreover are serving to occupy our citizens for a rapidly growing aggregate of hours per week, thereby effectively solving the social problems created by increasing surplus leisure time.

Before I proceed to statistics, it may be well to retrace briefly the development of the program that has so deeply affected our cultural infrastructure. In the 1950's, despite recommendations by President Eisenhower's Committee on National Goals that government manifest more interest in the arts, and despite the introduction of a bill into the 86th Congress providing for a Federal Advisory Council on the Arts, the government remained in a state of passive inactivity. With the change of Administrations, however, interest began to rise, with the result that the 87th Congress had before it some fifty bills, ranging from Senator Javits's proposal for an aid-giving United States Arts Foundation to Representative Anfuso's measure setting up a Department of Culture. A milestone was reached in the appointment of Mr. August Heckscher as Consultant on the Arts to the Executive Office of the President, and confidence was felt by a majority of the forward-looking persons in the Nation that our government would soon finalize its thinking and undertake full responsibility for furthering

the arts no less than it had done in respect to industry, agriculture, and labor, and the various subdivisions thereof.

Yet, despite such favorable auguries, and the remarkable instances of personal cultural interest and leadership provided by the White House under your Administration, effective steps of co-ordinated progress were to remain in abeyance for some time. It was not until the memorable events of 1965, in fact, that definite forward moves were made. For it was in that year, you will recall, that after a long struggle our major industries and labor unions agreed to adopt the twenty-hour work week, thereby advancing the cause of American leisure but also raising the question of what activities would best serve to fill the newly attained free time.

It was then that the present program of all-out governmental support of the arts took practical and effective legislative shape under the memorable slogan, "Fight boredom by improving the mind." First, under the impact of the emergency, we saw the creation of the Interim Cultural Co-ordinating Commission to survey the needs and recommend prompt action to relieve the new threat to America—free time on hand with nothing to engage it but television and baseball. I cannot too highly commend our major labor unions for having brought this issue to a head, for it resulted in what we in the Department call our general cultural breakthrough. Departmentally it was realized that far-reaching pursuits and participation in the arts and crafts field, Federally aided, would serve as massive deterrents to social waste and disorder. The 89th Congress, rising to the challenge, enacted the historic National Cultural Redevelopment Act and also created the Department of Arts and Leisure, which under its first Secretary, Mr. Heckscher, embarked upon the extensive program that I have the honor to continue.

Thus, under the Act, we have the Poetry Relief Program, which grants tax exemption to self-employed writers of verse who may qualify, and thus has enormously increased the number of our

By WILLIAM HARLAN HALE

A MEMORANDUM

To: The President

From: The Secretary of Arts and Leisure

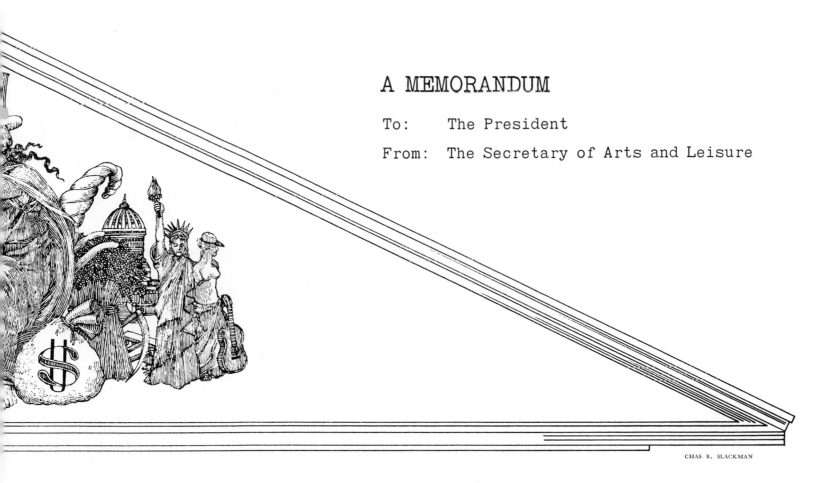

CHAS B. SLACKMAN

poets. (Since it seems still to be deplorably true that more people want to write poetry than read it, the question is now raised of how to dispose of the Federally aided poet's work. A committee of surplus experts formerly associated with the Department of Agriculture is now at work on the problem.) We have the Culture Credit Corporation, operating with a revolving fund of $100 million in the last year to buy and store various art products in such a way as to establish a price "floor" under them. We also have the Federal Art Encouragement Board, which in the last year granted 5,871 scholarships to abstract painters and 181 to non-abstract painters. All their works, of course, will be sent abroad under the joint aegis of the State Department, the Arts and Leisure Department, and the United States Information Agency for distribution in the undercultured areas of the world. It is my firm belief that by such methods as these, in addition to spurring creativity, full employment, and art appreciation at home, we may materially alter America's cultural image abroad and convert it from the debit to the credit column in the international ledger.

Your own decisive actions have had no little impact on the morale and what may be termed the on-going philosophy of the Department. In this connection I might mention your firm stand against the proposed merger of the National Gallery and Guggenheim Museum, your last-minute cancellation of the Central Intelligence Agency's plan to subvert the entire cast and artistic direction of the Bolshoi Ballet, and your courageous intervention when the domestic art-supply industry attempted to raise the price of pastel crayons. The stirring phrase from your Second Inaugural—"The culture of America is culture"—has been an inspiration to all of us who play a part, however minor, in the struggle for national aesthetic security.

Finally, I cannot forbear mentioning the Federal Country Music and Folk Ballads Institute, set up with a contributing grant by the Ford Foundation. We also have the Permanent National Dance Festival, again assisted by various foundations, and the Little Lincoln Center Program (reproductions of New York City's center to be erected in every American community in the ten to fifty thousand population bracket with matching Federal, state, and local funds under the slogan, "Fall-out shelters for the human spirit"); and there is, in addition, former Senator William Benton's program for continuous twenty-four-hour-a-day piped-in symphony music for all higher-education institutions, at only a nominal charge to the government.

Naturally such revolutionary and future-oriented developments in a sector of the national life of paramount significance to every citizen cannot be effected without adverse comment from partisan political quarters. It is perhaps no coincidence that Committees from both houses of the Congress are currently investigating the alleged overconcentration of Federal funds for literary study at Harvard, and what are claimed to be irregularities attending the award of last year's Pulitzer Prize for Poetry to a former official in the Journalism Review Board. I can only say that all the members of the Department were greatly concerned at any embarrassment caused by the unfortunate incident of the overzealous division chief in Fort Worth, Texas, who purchased—for purposes of stockpiling—four hundred fraudulent Renoirs.

In sum, Mr. President, I think I may say that we are pushing forward concertedly on every sector of our cultural front, and in a manner that bids fair to overcome past lags. We still labor, to be sure, under the handicap of an appropriation that in the last fiscal year granted only $430 million for so far-reaching a program; but I trust, Mr. President, that an enlightened Congress will see fit in the forthcoming year to raise its sights to a level more concomitant with American greatness.

Respectfully yours,
Cadwallader Stufflebeam
Secretary of Arts and Leisure

19

AN ORIENTAL PALACE

FOR AN ENGLISH KING

Pointing at the Sussex clouds, but suggesting aspirations higher, the skyline of Brighton Pavilion's East Façade shows off its Indian minarets, onion domes, and narrow towers, all rising above an adaptation of Islamic bay windows and entrances. These Oriental fancies were brought into an 1800 Occidental setting by the architect of Regent's Park, John Nash, working under the immediate supervision of George, Prince Regent. The building, which displays almost classically Georgian proportions and symmetry, took some thirty-five years to complete and is of mainly honey-colored Bath stone and stucco. This aquatint is one of a series of "Views" produced by Nash at the command of the Prince Regent soon after the latter ascended the throne to become George IV.

By J. H. PLUMB

The amorous, exuberant George IV, when still Prince Regent, began building a retreat to suit his own fancy. Result: Brighton Pavilion, perhaps the most exotic extravaganza to survive time's decay

Today, Brighton is Britain's Miami—brash, extravagant, a curious mixture of vulgarity and elegance, sophistication and naïveté, where literary lions, juvenile delinquents, successful *nouveaux riches,* and proletarian Cockneys out on a spree jostle in a lively, garish world that possesses one of the most remarkable architectural settings of any seaside resort in Europe. Throughout the length and breadth of Brighton there are squares, terraces, crescents of exquisitely classical proportions, rivaled in England only by Bath and in Europe only by Nancy. There is no whimsey about these buildings; the only exoticism is an occasional decoration in the neo-classical style of the late eighteenth and early nineteenth century. And then, lying in the very heart of this formal beauty, close to the seashore but set back from it, is the fantasy of the Brighton Pavilion—with its domes and minarets, its fretwork tracery and lacelike embattlements; and underneath this Oriental masquerade, the fine proportions of Henry Holland's classical villa, the first Pavilion, can still be discerned, as Georgian and as classical as any house in Brighton. It was built by the Prince Regent (1762–1830), the eldest son of George III, and like the Prince the Pavilion grew more monstrous, more extraordinary, more dreamlike with the years. But first, why should the Pavilion be found in Brighton?

Two hundred and fifty years ago Brighton scarcely existed —a few fishermen's hovels, a shingle beach, and right to the shore, smooth undulating grasslands that rose within a mile or so to the sharp escarpment of the Downs. It was excellent country for the horse, for riding it, racing it, or driving it. And that, later, was one of the reasons for Brighton's popularity, for many of the Prince's friends were crazed about horses as only the English aristocracy can be. But Brighton first grew to fame and fashion through the salesmanship of a successful doctor. He sold sea water. Its virtues, said Dr. Russell, whether applied externally or internally, were boundless. A cold dip, it seemed, proved peculiarly efficacious to that feminine frailty of the age of elegance—the vapors—so long as it was taken at hideously inappropriate times: Fanny Burney, the novelist, bathed in November before dawn, a very good time, the doctors thought. Also, as might be expected, sea-bathing or sea-drinking encouraged fertility in young matrons, "better even," said its advocates, "than the mud of the river Nile."

The Prince Regent's first visit to Brighton—a short one—

took place in 1783 at the invitation of his uncle, the Duke of Cumberland, whom the Prince's father, George III, regarded with such horror that he had forbidden his son to visit him. As soon as the Prince was twenty-one, with his own establishment, and free to please himself, he had accepted Cumberland's invitation with alacrity. The visit proved hugely successful, for Brighton seemed to offer all that the Prince needed. He found Brighton gay, intimate, discreet. It was still too far from London for crowds to gather there: his own set could, and did, take over the place.

So Brighton became the Prince's playground. He and his friends were fond of vulgar and noisy practical jokes on their neighbors. Who could stop them in Brighton? They raced their horses and drove their phaetons in mad competition across the wide lawns that bordered the sea. No one was likely to complain. They sat at their telescopes and watched old Martha Gunn, the ladies' bathing attendant, known popularly as "Queen of the Dippers," help their favorite girls into the sea: after all, the girls were there for adventure, too. Occasionally the men even sat in the ice-cold water themselves when they thought their health demanded it. They gambled endlessly, gazed at plays, danced, listened with respect to the Prince's fine baritone as he regaled them with ballads, drank furiously, ate gigantically, and wenched interminably. And they dressed. The Prince possessed a handsome, florid face, a splendid, if slightly plump, figure, and first-class legs, of which he was inordinately proud. He was even prouder of his taste in clothes, formed and guided by his friend Beau Brummell, who had revolutionized the Englishman's dress by insisting on subdued colors, perfect cut, and exquisite linen as the marks of elegance. Only in the evening, on

full-dress occasions, were princes and nobles permitted to dress like peacocks. But clothes and the wearing of them was a matter for daily concern and long discussion.

Princes and their friends, after settling on a place like a cloud of butterflies, often gorge themselves on its nectar and then flutter away to stimulate their appetites in fresh pastures. This time, however, fate riveted the Prince to Brighton. He fell in love with a dangerously unusual widow—Mrs. Fitzherbert. Mrs. Fitzherbert was a Roman Catholic—pious, virtuous, very comely. She neither welcomed the Prince's attentions nor responded to his ardor. She preferred to be left alone. The Prince's siege grew hectic: he swore, he cajoled, he promised; presents rained on her, letters pursued her, finally marriage trapped her. Conducted in utmost secrecy, it was, of course, illegal. No prince of the British royal family could marry without the sovereign's consent; no consent could have been forthcoming from George III for a marriage to a Roman Catholic widow. On the Prince's part the ceremony was meaningless folly; on hers, the necessary religious sanction to her bedding with the Prince. In Mrs. Fitzherbert's eyes, and in the eyes of her Church and of her fellow believers, the Prince was her husband. In English law, she could be nothing but his mistress. The Prince, of course, flaunted his conquest but strenuously denied, even to a friend as close as Charles James Fox, the method by which he had achieved it. Nevertheless, rumors reverberated, and George III, never a man of easy temper, regarded his son with so prejudiced an eye that he left him to stew in his debts. During his frantic courtship the Prince, according to Lord Holland, had rolled in grief on Charles James Fox's floor, crying by the hour and "swearing that he would abandon the

Another in HORIZON's series on unique palaces and pleasances, which so far has presented the Turkish Sultans' Grand Seraglio (May, 1959), Bavarian King Ludwig II's rapt mansions (January, 1961), Marlborough's Blenheim (September, 1961). To come: the Escorial and Hadrian's Villa.

ALLEGORY

While building his pleasure-dome, the Prince Regent also pursued Mrs. Maria Fitzherbert, thus providing sport for cartoonists. Rowlandson drew the couple after their secret marriage, in a plumply comfortable pose (opposite, left); and a popular print, The Wedding Night or The Fashionable Frolic *(opposite, right) set them tripping to the fiddle of George Hanger, a friend of the Prince. In Rex Whistler's allegory (left), painted in 1944 and now hanging in the Pavilion, an angelic Prince awakens the slumbering spirit of—Brighton.*

country, forgo the crown, sell his jewels, and scrape together a competence to fly with her to America." Instead of which, once wed, he drove off in ostentatious austerity to Brighton and installed Mrs. Fitzherbert conveniently near the farmhouse that he had begun to regard as his own.

As soon as Parliament accepted the denials of the Prince's friends about his marriage, persuaded the King to grant him £10,000 more a year and to settle his debts, the Prince was able to devote himself to love, architecture, and interior decoration which, with food, drink, and music were to be the obsessions of his life. For more than forty years he pursued all of them at the Pavilion that he built for himself at Brighton, or rather, that he went on building at Brighton, for like all compulsive builders and decorators, the Prince was never finished. Indeed, when the Pavilion was at last completed, the Prince, by then King George IV, lost interest in it and gave his attention to Windsor, where, with both the Castle and the Royal Lodge on his hands, he could fully occupy both his old age and his regal income.

In 1785, when the Prince first took Mrs. Fitzherbert to Brighton to spend the summer in what they thought of as "abject poverty," he rented a small, neat farmhouse from Thomas Kemp, who afterwards built the splendid Georgian terraces of Kemptown. The Prince could not live in any building without letting his imagination begin to work on it. Already, his palace in London—Carlton House—had been more responsible than any other extravagance for his monumental debts. So in the intervals of his amorous delights, and when he was too tired for the crude practical jokes in which he took such schoolboyish delight, he paced about his farmhouse. In his mind's eye, he knocked down walls and threw out bow windows, transforming the modest construction into a charming marine pavilion, suitable for a prince wallowing in marital bliss. Within eighteen months, one hun-

dred and fifty workmen, under the direction of the Prince's architect, Henry Holland, had turned dream into reality. Holland's structure possessed the simplicity and elegance that Georgian architects achieved so effortlessly. Its central feature was a circular salon that was flanked by two wings with bow windows. The building veered toward austerity, and the only whimsey it contained was the Prince's bedroom where a vast mirror enabled the Prince, and presumably Mrs. Fitzherbert, to lie in bed and watch not only the sea but their friends strolling up and down the Steine, as the wide grass lawn of Brighton was called—a quaint, but no doubt restful, pastime.

The Prince's Brighton friends were an odd bunch: Beau Brummell, for example, lived for clothes and spent the entire day dressing, parading, undressing, and parading again— as fastidious and as pure in his private life as in the cut of his coat. Others, like Lord Barrymore, never washed; his own and his brother's fame rested partly on their practical jokes—propping up coffins in doorways, then ringing the doorbell, was a favorite—and partly on their wild extravagance, due mainly to excessive gambling and lavish theatricals. And then there was Letty Lade: anyone who was particularly foulmouthed the Prince would describe as swearing "like Letty Lade." She had lost her virtue to "Sixteen-String Jack," a highwayman hanged at Tyburn in 1774, enjoyed for a short time the bed of the Prince's brother, the Duke of York, and finally married Sir John Lade, who finished life supremely happy as a public coachman on the London-Brighton run.

Many of the Prince's friends were obsessed and ingrown characters. Great wealth and absolute social security combined to create a hothouse atmosphere in which human characters could flower like monstrous orchids—vivid, splotched, nightmarish, haunting. Brighton was for them a paradise, where for months on end they could forget the real world of lawyers, tradesmen, stewards, politicians, and above all, the threats and later the horrors of war.

The Prince and Mrs. Fitzherbert had begun their life in Brighton determined to live sparely. That resolution quickly vanished and his debts mounted: by 1795, to well over half a million pounds. Furthermore, there was no immediate heir to the throne. All his brothers either lived in sin or, like himself, had contracted marriages that no one would recognize: although George III had plenty of bastard grandchildren, the direct succession of his house seemed to be in jeopardy. And the Prince's love for Mrs. Fitzherbert had withered to habit and habit itself had grown brittle.

The solution to his financial difficulties was to marry a German princess, breed an heir, and allow a grateful country to discharge his debts and increase his income. The alternative was a personal crisis of monumental proportions which would almost certainly entail a sharp contraction in his style of living. He was far too middle-aged to face that. So he married. He loathed his strange bride and got through the marriage ceremony only by fortifying himself with brandy. His wife was dotty: a hoydenish, blowsy, free-speaking German wench who dressed in outrageous taste, swore like a hostler, and smelt like a farmyard. Or so the Prince and his friends said—at least it gave an excuse for the vile way he treated her. He managed, however, to get his Princess pregnant, and duty done and the daughter born, he turned the Princess out of his house but not out of his life. She careered around Europe in vulgar ostentation, as much to embarrass the Prince as to enjoy herself. Certainly the Prince's legal marriage was the most disastrous act of his life.

Once he had extricated himself from this horror, he naturally wished to re-create the years with Mrs. Fitzherbert, which now glowed in his imagination. Her pride bruised, she showed her former indifference, which once again fanned the Prince's ardor to fever heat. There was nothing like denial to raise the Prince's passion. After a becoming interval, Mrs. Fitzherbert sent a priest off to Rome for advice. It was apt: return to your husband. She did, and both returned to Brighton.

Not only did Mrs. Fitzherbert make the Prince supremely happy—the next eight years, she was to say, were the happiest in his life—she also made him creative. Again he began to play about with the Pavilion. In 1802 the gift of some Chinese wallpaper, received no doubt because he had created a Chinese room at Carlton House in 1801, gave him the idea of making not only a Chinese gallery at the Pavilion but a room with walls of painted glass which gave one the impression of being inside a Chinese lantern. For the next few years, shortage of money and the need to complete the stables (they cost £54,000—no horses, nor grooms for that matter, had ever been more splendidly housed) limited the Prince's ambitions, but the Pavilion was enlarged a little

and the interior decoration made more and more what the English thought to be Chinese. But the Prince was not satisfied, and he decided to reconstruct the Pavilion, to turn it from a princely cottage into a miniature palace, small in size, yet rich, fabulous, Oriental in decoration. Not a Chinese pagoda: the Prince was moving away from Chinese towards what he conceived to be an Indian style. Already at Sezincote in Gloucestershire, a nabob, returned with a huge fortune from India, had built himself an Oriental palace; fortunately for him, his brother—S. P. Cockerell—was an excellent architect who took his task very seriously and carefully used water-color drawings of actual Indian buildings. The result was strange but pleasing. William Porden, who built the stables at Brighton, had worked for Cockerell, and he used this exceptionally original style of decoration at Brighton. This entranced the Prince; in 1805, he commissioned Humphrey Repton to plan an Aladdin-like transformation of his classical marine villa into an Indian palace. The Prince praised the drawings but did not build. Once more, he was broke. And possibly he had doubts about Repton's scheme, which conformed very strictly to Indian models. Highly disciplined and rather dry in tone, it lacked, perhaps, the personal accent for which the Prince's imagination was searching.

He hesitated for another six years until, indeed, the final madness of his father made him king in all but name. Then he got hold of a regal income and began to build as no English king had ever built before. The encouragement he gave to John Nash, the Surveyor-General whom he personally appointed in 1815, made the Regent as responsible as anyone for the most beautiful domestic architecture London pos-

TEXT CONTINUED ON PAGE 29

The Bright Interiors of Brighton

John Nash designed the spacious rooms of the Royal Pavilion with exotic and sumptuous effect, and then made the aquatints on the following pages to record their look and life. Even his Great Kitchen (opposite, above) boasted palm leaf capitals, fashioned from sheet bronze, on its four supporting columns. The Stables (opposite, below) were capped by glass panes in the shape of lotus leaves and set in a soaring, quasi-Indian dome. Forty-four stalls ran in circumference around the exercising yard, which had an enclosed balcony above for hostlers and grooms.

Overleaf: In the largest and most ornate salon of the palace, the Banqueting Room, the Prince nightly indulged his huge appetite—he is seen at the center of the right side of the dining table, reaching for wine. Above him, the ceiling is painted as "an Eastern sky partially obscured by a luxuriant plantain tree"; a silver dragon clutches the gaslit chandelier.

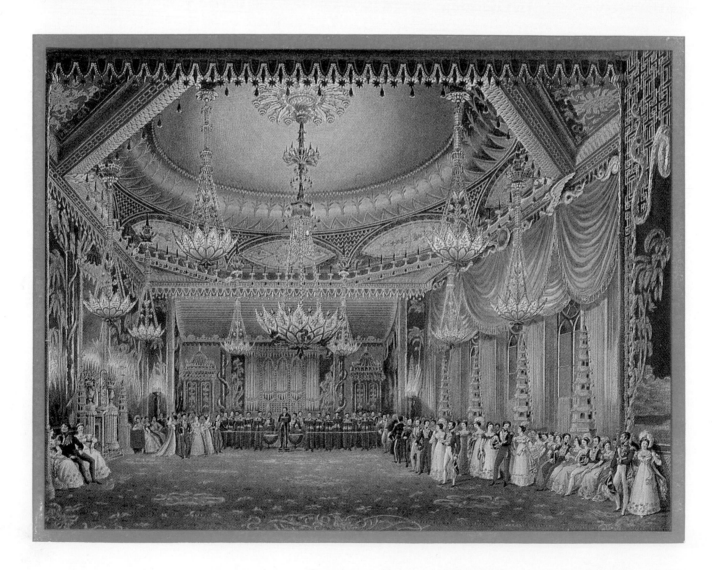

TEXT CONTINUED FROM PAGE 24

sesses—the great terraces of Regent's Park. Nash's Pavilion at Brighton, however, owed as much to the effects of time and experience on the Prince's character as to Nash's architectural genius. It was the final expression of his life. Every detail in decoration, furnishing, and color was personally supervised by the Regent and, if need be, changed time and time again until he judged it to be right. To understand the strange fantasy that came to life by Brighton's seashore, it is necessary to understand how time had changed the Prince.

By 1815 his youth had passed; Mrs. Fitzherbert had been rejected a second time. Indeed, another reason for his delay in reconstructing the Pavilion was the change in direction of his amorous life, which kept him away from Brighton for a year or two. Gross in body, somewhat wandering in mind, prone to invalidism, the Prince was driven farther into his private dream world by the antics of his wife and the hatred of his subjects. At the visit of the crowned heads of the European alliance to London in 1815, his wife had returned to London and insisted on undertaking what she considered to be her rightful duties. The Regent was outraged and, this time supported by his mother, refused to countenance what he considered infamous behavior. The radical politicians denounced the Prince and the mob pelted him when he appeared in public, so that he became afraid to go out of doors. He knew himself to be a figure of contempt, and could banish age and a sense of decay only by shutting himself in a private world: a world of eating, drinking, singing, building, and decorating—shared with a few dependable friends and ruled by matriarchs. The first of these was Lady Hertford, the second Lady Conyngham—two enormous, elderly women, much older than himself, who could treat him as he wished to be treated, as a loveless, foolish boy to be scolded, pampered, bullied, and always forgiven.

Yet the Prince still possessed a saving grace. He needed to express himself, to create, to allow his imagination to roam. His nature, as his life showed, was deeply fissured

Embellishments inside the Pavilion were mostly of a style that might be called Chinese Gothic. The Long Corridor (opposite, above) which suffered several changes of design and coloring, had wallpapers upon which "exotic flowers unfolded their petals and humming birds disported themselves." Much of its furniture came from China, as did the lanterns, the trophies, and the life-sized statues in their silk robes and wall niches. The Eastern motif recurs in the Music Room (opposite, below) with its porcelain pagodas, its dragons and twining serpents, and its imitation-lacquer paintings in yellow and gold, brushed on to the red ground of a fine cambric linen. Here the Prince (seated, left, between his mistress Lady Conyngham and her daughter) would listen to an orchestra or military choir, such as this one; and here too he might occasionally sing for his guests.

with anxieties, frustrations, and other weaknesses that were hard to face. In fantasy he could be soothed: pretense with him easily became reality. He was a man of romantic imagination, with the impulse of an artist and the temperament of an actor. His strange nature found its most effective, if not its most satisfactory, fulfillment in building and decorating; and the two architectural fantasies of his broken old age—the final Brighton Pavilion and the restoration and rebuilding of Windsor Castle—are both in their way romantic masterpieces. Windsor, with its stupendous Round Tower, is central to the tradition created by the Gothic Revival, but Brighton, when completed, had neither past nor future. Outside, Indian and Moorish mingled with the eighteenth-century elegance of sash and bow windows to create a unique building that baffled the understanding as much as it stimulated the imagination. The Pavilion is a dream, belonging neither to Russia nor India nor China nor Mongolia nor to Moorish Spain, but to the Prince's longing for a smart originality that would astound his friends. The inside, like the outside, is a strange pastiche, at times, with its strong reds and yellows and blues, almost vulgar, yet never quite. On first viewing, it is overpowering and slightly repellent: the huge lotus-like chandeliers, the dragons writhing down the walls, the imitation blue skies, palms in cast iron, banana trees in bronze, seats pretending to be dolphins, and everywhere bamboo chairs, bamboo beds, bamboo bookcases, bamboo seats (but, of course, imitation bamboo—even bamboo in iron). The Pavilion shocks as few other buildings do; it creates immediately the atmosphere of a life, the true setting for the man who made it. It is easy to imagine these rooms grossly overheated, to see again the vast kitchen teeming with Gargantuan piles of food and noisy with sweating cooks and scullions, orchestrated by Carême, one of the greatest of French chefs, to provide excitement for the palates of the twenty or so old roués, and their wives or mistresses, who sat with the Prince in his Banqueting Room. This room and the Music Room are the two most extravagant and extraordinary rooms not only in the Pavilion but in Great Britain.

The Banqueting Room (see pages 26–27) is dominated by its central chandelier—a vast structure in 1818—immensely modern because it was lit by gas, not candles. It weighs a ton and consists of a bronze-leaved plantain tree from which hangs a large silver dragon holding in his claws an enormous glass bowl; around its rim are six smaller dragons with lotus flowers in their mouths. The cost was £5,613..9s. (multiply by ten for present prices in pounds sterling and by thirty for dollars). The Prince took advantage of all the technical achievements of his time: the Pavilion is the first house to use cast-iron pillars both for structure and decoration. He loved light as well as heat, so, besides this huge chandelier, there are four other enormous water lilies and eight ten-foot-high standard lamps—a pedestal of gilded dolphins, a huge, deep blue Spode vase topped by a lotus flower of tinted glass (cost: more than five thousand

29

pounds). The room itself is painted with Chinese scenes; the décor is crimson, gold, and blue. The decorative work cost more than eight thousand pounds, and the furniture nearly ten thousand. The total expense of this single room was the equivalent of about one million dollars. (The entire Pavilion cost about £500,000 in gold, the equivalent of fifteen million dollars today.)

Certainly Carême's meals were worthy of it. The richness of the dishes was matched only by their number. At a dinner of no particular importance the Prince, greedier than ever, offered the guests the choice of one hundred sixteen dishes in nine courses. He adored the table, not only for the food and wine, but also because while he remained at table, his audience was captive. There, among the silver and the glass and the hissing gaslight, in a room that might have been Samuel Goldwyn's idea of the Summer Palace at Peking, he told of the battles he had never fought, the women he had never possessed, and the triumphs he had never known. There he was, a huge mass of flesh, corseted, bedecked, corrupted by his life and nature, yet retaining, even in decay, an originality and something of the singularity of the artist. His outrageous stories were so vivid that his audience—softened by good food and excessive drink—could at least *pretend* without difficulty to believe them. When in top form or reckless with drink, he took to mimicry. Then he entered so wholeheartedly into the subject of his satire that his huge face and vast body seemed to transform themselves even into the lean figure and hatchet face of a Wellington or the austere, arrogant good looks of his minister, Sir Robert Peel.

When tired, at last, of the table, the Prince withdrew with his guests into one of the three small drawing rooms which had been the heart of Holland's villa. Here, as in the Long Corridor (page 28), the decoration is restrained and restful, the colors soft and delicate and rare. But beyond this suite of drawing rooms lies the second wonder of the Pavilion—the Music Room (page 28). It was of this room that Princess de Lieven wrote, "I do not believe that, since the days of Heliogabalus, there has been such magnificence and such luxury. There is something effeminate in it which is disgusting. One spends the evening half-lying on cushions; the lights are dazzling; there are perfumes, music, liqueurs." (As might be expected, the Prince loved perfumes and cases of quart bottles were constantly being sent to Brighton.)

The room seems to recall Marco Polo's description of the great tent of Ghenghis Kahn. As in that, serpents writhe head-first down the columns which divide the great red lacquer panels painted in gold with Chinese scenes. The great convex ceilings of the recesses have roofs of beribboned bamboos. The central ceiling is a vast dome, decorated with diminishing scales. Flying dragons abound, and the central chandelier is a vast Chinese water lily. Again the cost was prodigious and the result fabulous. In this room the Prince held his formal concerts at which Rossini and Kelby sang. Here, too, the Prince rendered his ballads in his dramatic baritone, now a little uncertain with age and drink, yet performed with *brio*.

Some of the most beautiful though far less impressive rooms of the Pavilion are the private apartments of his brother, the Duke of Clarence, who afterwards became King William IV, and those of the Prince's ill-fated daughter, Princess Charlotte, who, much to the Prince's grief, had died in childbirth in 1817. In these the scale is domestic, the colors delicate, and the Chinese and Oriental motifs give a gaiety and a difference to rooms that are essentially in the English Regency style. They illustrate, as the public rooms do, the Prince's exceptionally fine sense of color, for he had them painted time and time again until he achieved the perfection he sought.

Although architecturally the Pavilion escaped into fantasy, it never extricated itself from the heart of Brighton. The Prince had bought land and houses at outrageous prices to make room for his stables and to give himself some privacy, but his gardens remained small, the front lawns scarcely bigger than those of a large villa. And even as the Pavilion was achieving its final form, Brighton was speedily changing. Roads, carriages, even horses, had undergone as rapid an improvement as the motorcar was to undergo in our time. By 1810 a day's visit to Brighton from London was common and not in the least difficult. The intimate privacy that the Prince had enjoyed with Mrs. Fitzherbert belonged to the remote past. And naturally, as Brighton became more middle-class, the aristocracy began to look elsewhere for its playgrounds.

However, before royalty and aristocracy finally left Brighton, it enjoyed a quaint Indian summer. After 1822, the visits of the Prince (now the King) grew less frequent: he was more and more addicted to the privacy which only the vast park at Windsor could give him. After his death in 1830, he was succeeded by his brother, the most outspoken, simple, eccentric, British monarch of modern times: William IV had been bred a sailor and he loved Brighton, loved to strut up and down the pier as if it were his own quarter-deck, loved even better having his own cronies in to dinner at the Pavilion, utterly oblivious to the Oriental magnificence that surrounded him. His Queen Adelaide, as homely as her husband, sat patiently at her embroidery and worried so much about the weight of the chandeliers that the King finally ordered the one in the Banqueting Room to be taken down. The resulting gap in the ceiling did not disturb either of them.

The guests of William and Adelaide needed to be prepared for shocks: one evening, when the band struck up a country dance to celebrate the New Year, the King seized Lord Amelius Beauclerk, a retired Admiral of the Fleet, and cavorted with him, hand in hand, down the Music Room. And then there was the even more electrifying occasion when the King stood up and said, "Now, ladies and gentlemen, I

ful triumphs the whole Spanish "way of life" was being undermined by a more successful rival ideology that had its headquarters in Amsterdam, the capital of those insubordinate, invincible, unpardonable heretics and rebels, the Dutch.

*F*or the Spanish peace had, in some respects, represented the victory and spread of a way of life. It was the triumph of princely bureaucracy, of an official class in a monarchical society, living to a large extent on taxes which grew as it grew. This official class had by now an official ideology, an ideology of the court: an ideology shared even by the great merchants, who farmed the taxes and felt themselves half courtiers; and consecrated by the Church, which was a court-Church, and particularly by the religious orders— most of all by the courtliest of all orders, the Jesuits, who at this time were the invariable allies of Spain. Such a system had its outward charm, of course. The bureaucracy patronized official art and architecture; it advertised itself and its solidity through magnificent buildings, which we admire today, and magnificent shows and pageants, which dissolved overnight. But it also had its weakness. Though it created a form of state-capitalism, it discouraged private trade and industry. Everywhere we see the same spectacle: industry and commerce crushed under bureaucracy; merchants shifting their capital into the purchase of land, titles, or offices; peasants oppressed by taxes; craftsmen fleeing to other lands.

This "Spanish" way of life was not confined to the Spanish empire, or even to Catholic countries. Wherever Spanish influence was felt, it was encouraged. We see it in France, the France of Marie de Médicis; we see it in England, the England of James I and the Duke of Buckingham. But over against it there was another way of life, the ideology of the country opposed to the court: of country landlords opposed to court magnates, of lesser merchants opposed to the great monopolists of the court, of taxpayers opposed to tax-eaters. This ideology was conservative: it was nationalistic, for it opposed an international system; it was anti-Spanish, and anti-clerical, for that system was operated by Spain and Rome; and against the ostentatious consumption of the court, it was "puritan." This ideology had been suppressed—indeed could hardly exist— in Spain and Spanish Italy; it seethed below the surface in England and France; but in Venice and Holland, in different forms, it ruled. Against Venice and Holland, therefore, all the hatred of Spanish officialdom was directed.

ish ambassador, the Count of Gondomar, arrived in London and completely captivated the court. For ten years the English court hung attentively on Spanish wishes. In 1618 Gondomar achieved his greatest public triumph when, at his request, the old Elizabethan Sir Walter Raleigh was sent to the block for trespassing in the now closed transatlantic empire of Spain. Even Protestant Holland, in those years, was under a pacific administration. It was because France, England, and Holland all moved in the Spanish orbit that Spain had been able to win those bloodless victories. And in 1621 France and England moved obediently in that orbit still. Why then were the ambassadors and viceroys so determined to break the Spanish peace?

The answer is not difficult to find. It is to be found in their own statements. These men believed that, in spite of appearances, Spain was losing the peace. This loss was not a loss of territory (Spanish territory had been constantly increasing), nor even merely a loss of trade (Spanish trade had never been much). It was something far greater than this. Beneath the surface of spectacular peace-

The Thirty Years' War strengthened France, weakened Spain, broke up the Hapsburg combine, and made the Holy Roman Empire little more than a name. But its chief effect was the ruin of Germany by a generation of violence. The losses were immense, even taking into account later exaggeration and the claims of propaganda (a legend grew up that Germany lost three quarters of its population, although it was probably closer to one third—still catastrophic). Whole regions lay desolated. For three decades, as in Callot's etching below, villages had been burned, women carried off, sons conscripted, crops destroyed, and livestock stolen by the marauding armies. In their train came famine and disease. It is no wonder that in 1628 a peasant wrote in his daybook: "God send that there may be an end at last; God send that there may be peace again. God in Heaven send us peace."

Of course, if the Spanish peace had really been consolidating Spanish power in Europe, there would have been no need for action: Spain could have waited till the dwindling "puritan" generation had died out. But the Spanish officials were convinced that time was not on Spain's side. They believed that the purpose of peace was to recover from the bankruptcy of war, to renew military strength, to create new resources for final victory. And that, it was only too clear, had not been done. Behind the façade of its wealth and strength, Spain had sunk deeper into bankruptcy, deeper into feebleness. Meanwhile its old enemies were using the peace to grow in power and prosperity. The courtly clerical, aristocratic system of Spain might be magnificent, but it did not work. The ideology of the Dutch might be heretical, rebellious, vulgar, but it worked. Time therefore was on their side. Fortunately, said the Spanish officials, the balance of power was still on the side of Spain, provided Spain struck, and struck now.

The Count of Gondomar, ambassador in England, wrote home in 1616 expressing his views at length. Unless the Spanish government made better use of the peace, he said, "I consider that war would be much better for the Catholic religion and the state and monarchy of Spain." Thanks to the peace, the English were increasing their trade and wealth and were becoming rich at the expense of Spain, which, for all its American mines, was now the poorest country in Europe: Spain brought gold and silver from overseas "only to distribute it among all the nations of the world, whose ships wait to carry it home." If Spain wished to win the peace, then, said Gondomar, it must adopt a new and positive policy. It was not enough merely to enjoy the respite, to relax and maintain a static system. Spain must invest in commerce, encourage shipping, found trading companies, abolish inland tolls, give a new status and new facilities to merchants. In this way trade and wealth would grow, shipping would be increased, and sea power would give ultimate victory in war, "for the world today is such that whosoever rules the sea rules the land also." But if Spain would not adopt this policy, then, said Gondomar, the proper course was war and war at once.

That was in 1616. Two years later, when he went home on leave, Gondomar was disillusioned with Spain. He could hardly recognize his country, he said: the poverty and depopulation of Spain compared with the wealth and activity of England and Holland was terrifying; he despaired of mastery of the sea. "England and

Holland have won the peace: we have lost it." But if the Spanish navy was rotted with disuse, the Spanish armies were still invincible, and the same argument was taken up, with a difference, by other more military-minded speakers. Such was Carlos Coloma, governor of Cambrai, who submitted his views in 1620 and 1621.

In 1609, he wrote, the Spaniards had made the truce because they supposed that peace would relieve their treasury and gradually dissolve the martial spirit and rickety government of the Dutch. But had it done so? On the contrary, the Dutch had made covert war on Spain in Venice and Germany, had captured the trade of East and West Indies, and had built up in twelve years an empire such as had cost the Portuguese and Spaniards one hundred and twenty years. Amsterdam, forty years ago "an almost unknown village," had become a world city eclipsing Genoa for wealth, Lisbon for merchandise, Venice for situation. "I conclude," wrote Coloma, "that if in twelve years of peace they have undertaken and achieved all this, we can easily see what they will do if we give them more time." Therefore, he urged, let Holland be destroyed. To des-

prolonged. "We must suppose," he protested, "that even if all Europe is destined to be subject to one monarch, that time is not yet." But as the old rulers died off, the new prevailed; and besides, they had other allies. The Councils of Portugal and the Indies, representing the East and West India trades, agreed with Zúñiga and Coloma. Those men had long suffered from the Dutch. In the years of the war the Dutch had seized half the East Indies from Portugal; in the years of peace they had stolen the trade of the West Indies. It was vain to hope of defeating them at sea, but a well-aimed blow by land would solve the problem. Struck in the heart, the octopus would loosen its distant tentacles. Thanks to this argument, and this support, the party of war prevailed. The truce was denounced. The half-settled troubles of Germany were swept up into a general war.

*T*hus we can answer our question. The Thirty Years' War, as a general war, was not created by the Bohemian and German incidents which officially began it. These could have been settled, or at least localized, as so many other such incidents had been. Perhaps no general war ever arises out of mere incidents. General wars arise because the governments of great powers, or the men behind such governments, want war and exploit incidents. In 1914 the German government did not want war, but the German General Staff did. In 1939 Hitler wanted war. And in 1621, in the greatest power in Europe, behind the politicians of the peace, there was a body of men—grim, faceless officials, contemptuous of political reasons—who positively wanted war because they believed that they could win the war whereas, in a modern world, they could not win the peace. It only remains to say that (as in 1914, as in 1939) they did not in fact win the war either. They began well, of course. They were prepared and their enemies were not. And they had chosen a good time. In the next few years the House of Hapsburg would win triumph after triumph and Spanish statesmen would dream of dominion over the Baltic and of the conquest of England. But then, slowly but effectively, the other great powers would be roused; war would reveal new forces, new techniques; once again Spain would be forced to make peace; and this time it would not be a Spanish peace: it would be the end of Spain as a great power.

H. R. Trevor-Roper, who frequently writes on historical subjects for HORIZON *(see "The Two Worlds of Don Quixote," November, 1961) is Regius Professor of Modern History at Oxford.*

troy it would be easy (Osuna had thought it would be easy to destroy Venice, Gondomar to destroy England): with England and France neutral, one campaign, one blitzkrieg would do it; but it must be done now.

In Madrid Coloma's arguments were driven home by Baltasar de Zúñiga himself. It seemed to him as if the Spaniards had shed their blood only to fill the veins of subject nations: "We have left our own country deserted and sterile in order to people and fertilize the lands we have conquered." Therefore, the Carthage on the Zuider Zee must be destroyed: the treasure of Spain that had been secretly drained away to the north must be brought back by force. Was it not for this day that Zúñiga himself and his fellow imperialists had worked so hard, throughout the Spanish Peace, to secure the vital corridors—the Valtelline, Alsace, the Palatinate? Now they had secured them all. Were they then not to strike?

When these arguments were first advanced in Madrid, there was resistance. How, men asked, could Spain face the cost of war? With his dying voice, the Archduke in Brussels urged that the truce be

THE MUSIC OF FRIENDS

Symphony orchestras, not to mention opera singers, make more noise—but string quartets have all the fun

Ever since chamber music emerged late in the sixteenth century, probably in Italy, it has been written primarily for amateurs, played mainly by amateurs, and kept alive by amateurs. If it is often performed by people whose enthusiasm outstrips their technique, they sometimes reach a subtle psychological rapport and inner harmony rarely attained by celebrated virtuosos, tempestuous prima donnas, or, for that matter, the frustrated second trombonist of a major symphony orchestra. I know professional musicians who consider their art merely a competitive business in which the fastest and loudest man wins. The true chamber-music player is not interested in an orgy of sound; he never wants to play louder than anyone else.

Few other ways of pursuing happiness are as stimulating and rewarding, as exciting and relaxing, as playing string quartets with congenial fellow players. Chamber music is more than a hobby: it is a lifelong passion. Personally, I have remained an incurable addict ever since I began as a lowly second fiddler at the tender age of eleven, and that was forty-four years ago.

But what exactly is the object of this addiction? The term *musica da camera* was originally used for music to be played at home—probably in the chamber of an aristocratic patron—rather than in church or at the opera house. Its distinguishing characteristic was the playing of individual parts by a single instrument, but the borderlines are somewhat blurred. Sonata teams are generally not considered to be chamber-music players: on the other hand, the lovely Mozart duos for violin and viola are certainly chamber music, and very fine, too. Madrigal groups are often rejected ("not instrumental enough"), while a small orchestra playing Bach or Handel often qualifies. (*Hausmusik,* a term often used for popular music played by small groups, is not considered chamber music by the purists. A trio arrangement of Rossini's *William Tell* overture or of tunes from *My Fair Lady* may be fun when played at home, but it isn't strictly chamber music.)

Two players are usually the minimum and about ten the maximum in chamber music, and quartets, quintets, and trios are the most popular groupings. Pianists are welcome so long as they behave with restraint and don't bang away like soloists. Flutists, oboists, clarinetists, and horn players will be invited occasionally into the circle, and there exist wood-wind and brass chamber groups.

Primarily, however, it is music for strings. During the Renaissance the "chest of viols," a set of six matched instruments—two treble, two tenor, two bass—became synonymous with chamber music. By 1660, when the great instruments made by the Amatis of Cremona were widely admired, the violin assumed its regal place in chamber music. In London, John Jenkins (1592–1678) issued his "Twelve Sonatas for Two Violins and a Base with a Thorough Base for the Organ or Theorbo." In the diaries of John Evelyn and Samuel Pepys we read of the enthusiasm of London society for chamber music, which was played in clubs run by John Banister and Thomas Britton or in private homes. "There was also much music making, on a rather lower social plane, in inns and taverns all over the country," writes the English musicologist A. Hyatt King, but this sort of music was mostly performed by professionals.

Three Connecticut neighbors join Leopold Godowsky in his study for an evening of chamber music. Paul Bernard, concertmaster of the Connecticut Symphony, is first violin; Andrew Petryn, art conservator at Yale, second violin; and Mrs. Marie Rosanoff, who has studied with Casals, cello. Godowsky, himself an accomplished violinist and the coinventor of Kodachrome, is on this occasion playing the viola.

By JOSEPH WECHSBERG

To play like the Budapest Quartet is every amateur's goal—remote, unattainable, but there. *From the left, its laughing members are: Alexander Schneider, Mischa Schneider, Joseph Roisman, Boris Kroyt.*

On the Continent chamber music was kept alive during the eighteenth century mainly by aristocratic amateurs. Many aristocrats who had learned to play an instrument supported professionals whose various duties included composing chamber works (with a good part for the master, to be sure) and attending to the music needs of the chapel and the ballroom. Prince Nicholas Esterházy, who employed Joseph Haydn until 1790, was known as a good baryton player (the baryton was a large viol with six or seven strings), and Haydn wrote one hundred twenty-five trios for baryton, viola, and bass in which he first tried out some of the experiments that he later brought off so gloriously in his string quartets.

Frederick William II, king of Prussia, was an able cello player who is now remembered for commissioning both Carl Gotthard Langhans to build the Brandenburg Gate and Wolfgang Amadeus Mozart to write six string quartets. Mozart completed three, K. 575, 589, and 590, and I daresay they will survive the Brandenburg Gate. Mozart succeeded in writing "grateful" cello parts for the King, using the other instruments to compensate volume and achieve architectural balance. Haydn, also, dedicated several quartets to the cello-playing King. And when His Majesty didn't play works especially written for him, he could always fall back on compositions by Allegri, Scarlatti, Tartini, Pachelbel, Buxtehude, the Stamitzes, and F. X. Richter.

After 1800 feudal patronage of chamber music continued to thrive in Vienna, where the Hapsburg court, local aristocrats, and princes of the church were all great enthusiasts. The names of Prince Schwarzenberg, Prince Lobkowitz, and Prince Nikolai Galitzin today live in the quartet dedications of Beethoven; and Count Andreas Rasumovsky has been immortalized by Beethoven's three "Rasumovsky" quartets, Opus 59. There is still a Palais Rasumovsky

in Vienna, and a latter-day Count Andreas Rasumovsky is now music critic of the *Frankfurter Zeitung*.

In 1808 the earlier Count Rasumovsky, Russian ambassador in Vienna and one of Beethoven's aristocratic friends and admirers, asked Ignaz Schuppanzigh, a local virtuoso, to form a regular quartet of professional musicians for the Count's musical soirees. Little did the Count know that he was making history, but chamber music has never quite recovered from the shock: once the exclusive domain of the amateur, it was now performed by technically skillful professionals who eventually moved out of the palace into the concert hall. Beethoven in his later years—and most nineteenth-century composers after him—wrote chamber music for these professionals, with the result that many of their works became so difficult that few amateurs were able to bring them off gracefully. Purists still feel that chamber music belongs in the home; but though it has remained divided between small groups of highly polished professional players performing in concert halls and large masses of well-meaning amateurs making music at home, the division has not been inimical: the best (though not always the most famous) professional quartets have something of the happy spontaneity and the divine improvisation that is the heart of chamber music, while ambitious amateurs get from the professionals an idea of how the works which they play at home ought to sound.

Chamber-music concerts are no longer the privilege of the selected friends of an aristocratic patron. It has been argued that the democratization of chamber music has diluted its very essence while broadening its limits, but it has also created an entirely new class of amateur addicts who love this music. And though feudal patronage ended with the decline of the old aristocratic society, patronage by wealthy, enthusiastic amateurs has remained. In Russia it was M. P. Belaiev (1836–1904)—devotee, publisher, and concert promoter—who made his home a chamber-music center; he was later rewarded when Rimsky-Korsakov, Liadov, Borodin, and Glazunov each contributed one movement to a quartet that was linked by a theme based on the syllables of his name, "Be" (B flat), "La" (A), and "Ef" (F). In England Walter Willson Cobbett (1874–1937), an enthusiastic amateur, revived the seventeenth-century tradition of short, one-movement pieces; the English countryside is now full of happy amateurs. In Western and Central Europe chamber-music concerts are sponsored by municipalities and large groups. In the United States Mrs. Elizabeth Sprague Coolidge and other patrons have stimulated chamber music by organizing festivals and series of concerts, awarding prizes, commissioning compositions, even buying fine instruments for famous quartets and building auditoriums.

Since this is a country where the pursuit of happiness is efficiently organized from cradle to grave, it should surprise no one that a nonprofit group, the Amateur Chamber Music Players (at 15 West 67th Street, New York 23, N.Y.), exists for the sole purpose of bringing chamber-music players together. A rather serious magazine has called it "private insanity of the most delightful kind." At a time when gloomy prophets predicted that radio, recordings, and television would cast a blight upon music-making in the home, the number of cheerful lunatics is increasing. The A.C.M.P.'s 1961 Directory lists over four thousand happy inmates in this country and several hundred in more than fifty countries abroad, including a lonely cellist, Dr. Fausto Tesio, in Amman, Jordan, and a splendidly isolated violinist, Miss I. M. Knight, in Bulawayo, Southern Rhodesia.

The Directory lists all members by name, address, telephone number (most important), instrument, and rating. Each member grades himself, A for excellent, B for good, C for fair, D for etc. (probably meaning not-so-fair), and Pro. for professional. It is characteristic of chamber-music players' healthy sense of self-respect that there are relatively few D's in the directory. Players temporarily stranded in a place where a member is listed will be assured, by simply making a phone call, of an evening of chamber-music hospitality, an endearing combination of music, food, and talk. Although the A.C.M.P. is the largest organization of its kind, statistics and figures are meaningless in chamber music. Many of us are notorious individualists who refuse to join any group and prefer the anonymity of our dimly lighted music rooms. For each player listed in a directory there must be dozens of unlisted ones. I have no doubt that there are tens of thousands of amateur players in America, and there are large concentrations in Austria, Germany, Switzerland, England, and elsewhere. You find them in all walks of life.

It is no accident that the A.C.M.P. Directory does not give a player's occupation. We chamber musicians are not interested in the private standing or professional doings of our fellow players. I have played music with people for months without knowing their first names or asking what they did; the conversation after the session was always spirited and often controversial, mainly about missed rests, the trap after letter D, and didn't-we-play-that-allegro-too-fast, but it would never occur to us to talk about our economic or emotional problems. I have played with commercial travelers and unworldly artists, with spinsters and divorcées, with Nobel prize winners and housewives, with students and scholars, with tax collectors and tax evaders, with inventors and engineers, with general managers and file clerks. I have never played with croupiers, truck drivers, or undertakers, but maybe there are some chamber-music players among them.

There are small circles and large groups, but the best players have their regular quartets "regularity" based on the hope that next Friday all four will again be able to get together. The A.C.M.P. now recognizes "contact persons" who have the "willingness to arrange musical sessions or to make suggestions for visiting A.C.M.P. members." Every quartet has such a contact person, the group's anonymous hero, unafraid of making countless telephone calls to get a viola player in a hurry because the regular one can't come. Some people advertise and others ask around; eventually you meet somebody who plays chamber music and from then on you'll be in, especially if you are able to play the difficult viola part in Smetana's *From My Life*. And a good cellist who knows his music and doesn't play it too loud may even bring along his pipe or his dog.

Cellists and violists are rare nowadays. The inexorable law of supply and demand has reversed the sacred order of the past when the First Fiddle was king in his quartet. (In chamber-music parlance a fiddle is an instrument, but a First Fiddle is the person who plays the first violin part; chamber-music players have the mysterious gift of hearing certain capital letters.) Mothers, let your unmarried daughters study the cello. At worst, their heavy instrument will always be carried home by one of the sixteen Fiddles that seem to come for each Cello; at best, they will be swept off their dainty feet by a forceful First Fiddle.

The average audience at a symphony concert or at an opera performance contains hardly any people able to perform any of the orchestra or singing parts. But in the audience of a chamber-music concert there is always a large percentage of slightly frustrated fiddlers, violists, and cellists. Chamber-music amateurs, unlike other music lovers, are not satisfied merely to listen to recordings or broadcasts; no sooner have they heard a work than they want to sit down to perform it themselves. People who prefer strong tone colors and dramatic effects in their music are usually happier with symphony orchestras and military bands. Playing string quartets is an exercise in democracy and a study in humility, a truly civilized pastime. The secret of chamber-music making is to listen to your fellow players while you yourself are playing. Some people never learn it; let them join amateur orchestras or play sonatas with their wealthy aunts. A good string quartet, somewhat like a good champagne, must be a blend. When four amateurs manage to play together softly yet clearly so that each instrument can be heard and the texture of the music becomes transparent, they've got something. They have created a string quartet, perhaps the most sensitive of all musical instruments and a triumph of Western civilization.

*T*here is a widespread belief that chamber-music makers are long-haired musical intellectuals, bloodless esoterics, highbrows with a G string. But watch four amateurs in action, as they swerve constantly between heights of happiness when a movement comes off and depths of despair when it does not (which, I regret to say, happens more often), and you will instantly recognize them as musical thoroughbreds. In this status-seeking world of ours, chamber music is the last stronghold of the uninhibited idealist and the uncorrupted amateur who isn't trying to prove something—to himself or to anyone—but wants to make music for the sake of music.

I have seen it happen even with famous professionals, who enjoy an evening of chamber music as much as the lowly amateur. It is well known that all the giants—Heifetz and Stern and Menuhin and Primrose and Piatigorsky and Casals and many others—play string quartets when they *really* want to have fun. And they make mistakes too. I have heard them myself (though I won't give you spicy details).

Our "literature," as we call our repertoire, is not very large but it is very beautiful. Of the approximately two hundred and fifty quartets in existence most of us play less than half, but they keep us happily occupied. We disagree on practically everything else, but I think we all consider the eighty-four quartets by Haydn, the twenty-four by Mozart, and the seventeen by Beethoven our classical gold reserve. Around these standard works we build our programs. (I don't subscribe to the theory that anybody should drop in next Thursday night and that anything will be played that happens to come to our mind; I believe a quartet evening at home should be lovingly planned and the program carefully designed to please all participants.)

It is the habit among quartet players "to play oneself in" with a Haydn, but as you get on in chamber-musical life, you consider Haydn much more than a sort of glorified warming-up exercise. Haydn was a giant; not only did he invent the string quartet as we know it today, but he gave us an incredible number of finished masterpieces. Some of the universally beloved Haydns were later given names by anonymous players, and so we now have a "Bird," a "Lark," a "Frog," a "Rising Sun," and an "Emperor" quartet, the last one containing the inspiring melody that became the national anthem of both the Austrian monarchy and Germany. There are gems among the early Haydns, such as Opus 20, No. 4, or Opus 33, No. 3, and among the later ones I love particularly the magic beauty of the opening movement of Opus 74, No. 1, the Beethovenish scherzo in Opus 77, No. 2—in fact, the whole series of masterworks he wrote in Opera 76 and 77, sometimes very difficult and delicate.

I have never met a chamber musician who didn't love Mozart, particularly the "Hunt" and "Dissonant" quartets, or the last of the "famous ten," in F major. To bring them off, all four players must have a sound sense of musicality, a certain amount of technique, and genuine taste and style. Even famous professional quartets that triumph with technically far more difficult works have been sadly grounded by the deceiving simplicity and graceful perfection of a Mozart quartet.

Everybody admires Beethoven, but string players do not always agree about his quartets. There is an erroneous belief among some amateurs that Beethoven's first six quartets (Opus 18) are relatively easy; in many ways they are just as delicately demanding as Mozart's. Not many amateurs dare play the "Rasumovsky" quartets of the "middle" period, which are technically very difficult. They contain bravura passages for the first violin that Beethoven wrote to show off Herr Schuppanzigh's virtuosity, and which have since caused the decline and fall of many amateur First Fiddlers (although every cellist wants to play the first of the three because it begins with a cantilena for the cello).

I was past fifty before I approached the "late" Beethovens, but I don't regret having waited. They should be performed with reverence and dedication: they are the most beautiful music in the whole chamber literature and among the greatest works ever written. Enormously difficult, deeply moving, superbly rewarding, they should be played at the end of a quartet evening; nothing can top them—although sometimes we follow up with a shorter Mozart, whose heavenly genius is the perfect antidote after Beethoven's earthbound suffering.

Some chamber-music players find Schubert a little long and repetitious; they feel like the aforementioned Schuppanzigh, who told Schubert after playing the "Death and the Maiden" quartet: "This is no good, my friend, leave well enough alone and stick to your songs." But no one except a morose second fiddler can miss the enchantment of Schubert's wonderful A minor (some second fiddlers hate it because of the difficult arabesques with which they have to start). And the posthumous *Quartettsatz* in C minor, though only a fragment, shows the whole range of Schubert's genius.

Aimez-vous Brahms? Not all string players do because "he writes

for the piano" even when he writes string quartets. There is great beauty in the A minor quartet, though, and violists love it; the andante has some rhythmic traps, and at the allegretto of the Minuetto certain disaster is waiting for the first violin and the viola. Schumann is the problem child of most quartet players: his work is "not grateful," "not fiddle-like"; it takes place "all on the middle strings." The finest of his three quartets, in A major, has made martyrs out of some second fiddlers—and cellists don't like it either.

Almost everybody loves Dvořák, an ex-violist, who wrote beautiful parts for the viola; his music may not always be great but it is always grateful, as you will discover when you bring off the "American" (Opus 96) with a touch of the flamboyant, or the lovely first movement of Opus 61. Some readers may have noticed that I mention some works by key, others by opus number and some by name. Don't ask why; it's just one of chamber music's minor mysteries. For us "the Verdi" means Verdi's only string quartet, an exciting piece with plenty of *Rigoletto, Otello,* and even *Falstaff* in it. "The Debussy" and "the Ravel" are those two composers' solitary quartets, uncontested masterpieces of our literature. The Debussy is bewitching with its tone colors but full of rhythmic difficulties; the Ravel starts out easily enough but gets progressively difficult, with a bewildering 5/4 measure in the last movement.

And that brings me to modern chamber music. Most amateurs I know approach modern works with suspicion and awe. I am afraid our generation has not attained the familiarity with its composers that Frederick William II and his players had with Haydn and Mozart, or the Rasumovskys and Galitzins with their contemporaries Beethoven or Schubert (although Beethoven was not generally admired by musicians at that time, and the cellist Romberg got so angry about Opus 59, No. 1—now considered a cellist's dream—that he threw his part on the floor and stamped on it). Does that mean that our generation of amateurs is less open-minded toward its own composers? Perhaps. The awful truth is, however, that many modern chamber-music works pose almost impossible problems of intonation, rhythm, and ensemble playing. Often we have started valiantly to read one of these works only to give up, reluctantly, after a while—the result simply wasn't worth the effort. The consensus was that an evening of chamber music should be some fun, after all, not atonal drudgery. I also suspect that we sensed instinctively that something was missing. Too many of these new works are constructed with the brain, not composed with the heart. They can be appreciated but are rarely loved, and thus they miss the essential spirit of chamber music. For me there is more modern—or, I should say, timeless, true, absolute—music in the late Beethovens than in anything written since.

There are exceptions of course. Bartók's quartets are magnificent, but how many amateurs can play them? Benjamin Britten's second quartet is exciting *and* playable. Dohnányi, Hindemith, Milhaud, and Pfitzner should be tried—if you can convince your fellow players. Much modern chamber music has a national flavor: Kodály's Hungarian tone colors, Malipiero's and Casella's Italian *brio,* Poulenc's and Honegger's Gallic wit. There is no doubt that the average amateur today plays better than the nineteenth- or eighteenth-century amateur, but I agree with A. Hyatt King when he says,

"The technical standards of atonal and microtonal chamber music are severe, being, in fact, beyond the range of all save professional musicians or highly skilled amateurs."

Cheer up. You can always fall back on Mozart and Beethoven. And if you're lucky and can get two viola players next week, you'll have a wonderful evening playing Mozart's magnificent string quintets in G minor and C major and Bruckner's powerful F major quintet, which has the great spiritual depth that you find in his symphonies. And all chamber-music players, without exception, are happy to perform Schubert's C major string quintet (for two cellos), as moving as the late Beethovens, a work of symphonic scope and power, and splendid proof, if such were necessary, of what a great master was able to achieve with only five instruments.

String-quartet playing, by common agreement the most popular and most beautiful chamber-musical pursuit, is not always pure and perfect bliss. It suffers from a delicate human-relations problem caused by the harsh fact that two members of the quartet play the same instrument. Which means that one of the two has to play second fiddle.

There are no Second Fiddles. There are only reluctant First Fiddles who agree to play second, exceptionally, just tonight, to make a quartet possible. They approach their task with martyrdom and give the First Fiddle an acute feeling of guilt. Beware of people who are eager to play second: they often collapse in vivace and presto movements and surrender to three flats or four sharps. A genuine second violinist—one who contributes dedication, a sense of rhythm, and enough technique to master the traps of his part—is an unmixed blessing. He does not get nervous when he has to play all by himself (as in the beginning of the Verdi) or has a beautiful solo (as in the adagio of Beethoven's "Harp" quartet).

The viola and the cello supply additional problems. Despite the celebrated examples of Dvořák, Hindemith, and Primrose, many violists still suffer from an inferiority complex, which erupts some-times after hours of placid co-operation. But a genuine violist—not an ex-fiddler who seeks refuge behind the thicker strings of the viola —is proud of his instrument with its beautiful sound. To appease your Viola you can play the Smetana, which is beautiful anyway.

Cellists should be dealt with cautiously but firmly. They can play louder than anybody else in the quartet, but even their parts con-tain passages marked *ppp.* When they accuse the first violin of "having ruined that movement again," they should be asked to play the last movement of Beethoven's Opus 127, which is partly, and diabolically, written in the violin key. That will teach them a lesson.

Sheer modesty has kept me from discussing my own problems. Before arriving at the first violin, I served my apprenticeship playing second fiddle, and I've played the viola and even the cello though I prefer not to remember it. My formative years helped me to discover what the members of an amateur quartet have a right to expect from their first violinist. He should have enough personality, style, taste, and technique to perform the works he has chosen to play. He should not consider himself a "leader"—that's old-fashioned and went out with the previous generation—but, rather, *primus inter pares.* In many modern quartets the second violin part is almost as difficult as the first. The ideal amateur quartet should have no

Sisters (in both senses of the word) Mary Denis, Mary Mark, and Mary Anthony have played chamber music since childhood. Now, as the Immaculate Heart Trio, they have achieved a remarkable unity of style.

"stars." No one should outshine the others. There should be a healthy balance of power; disagreements should be discussed and settled by majority decision. Many disagreements are created by questions of speed. The violist wants to play the last movement as fast as he heard the Budapest do it, but the first violinist, who has the difficult runs, is reluctant—and the fight is on.

A quartet evening is always something of a calculated risk. One of the players arrives breathless, and his nervousness immediately affects the others. The first movement doesn't come off, because it was cold outside and the strings go down. Just as the first violin plays his beautiful cantilena, the doorbell or the phone rings. The lights are too bright, the room is too hot, the audience is noisy (the best evenings are those without listeners anyway). Everything goes wrong, and you begin to wonder whether the evening will be an utter failure.

And suddenly there is an inexplicable change. Suddenly every-body plays all the notes in the score and each player can hear his fellow players as well as himself. They no longer perform parts of a score but make music, which is not the same thing at all. Instead of just "bringing off" that movement, the players feel they have pene-trated beyond the surface into the very spirit of the music. Suddenly the room is filled with harmony and with the subtle rapport achieved by four people who are emotionally and melodiously in tune. It is in moments like this that you understand why chamber music has al-ways been called "the music of friends."

Joseph Wechsberg is one of the most ardent First Fiddles in Vienna, where he is now resident and where—between quartets —he frequently writes on musical and other subjects for HORIZON.

A Rouault self-portrait

THE PASSION ACCORDING TO ROUAULT

Hitherto unknown paintings reveal a master of religious art at the height of his powers

Georges Rouault, whom Jacques Maritain has called "one of the greatest religious painters of the ages," was born in Paris in 1871, the son of a cabinetmaker, and died in 1958, rich in honors and belated recognition. Though now ranked high among the masters of the modern movement, throughout his long life he belonged to no school and went his own way, painting the few subjects that interested him—judges, clowns, prostitutes, the Christ—and pursuing with a single-minded devotion his own ideal, an artist (in James Thrall Soby's phrase) "with a limited vision of unlimited ferocity."

The full measure of his fame did not come to him quickly. For many years the public, and even his friends and original admirers (like the ardent Catholic writer Léon Bloy), misunderstood him and ridiculed him for his "dark" pigments, his preoccupation with what seemed to them the sordid and the ugly. "You have," Bloy wrote him after one exhibition, "a vertigo of hideousness. . . . [A] man of prayer . . . could not paint these horrible canvases." Rouault's reaction was to conceal his hurt and persevere. He was in fact a man of intense, uncomplicated faith, and it was such a faith that sought and found expression in the somber intensity, the massive and brutal solidity, of his religious paintings, especially those on the theme of the Passion.

The Rouault paintings on the pages that follow are virtually unknown and have never before been published. They are among the originals, soon to be exhibited publicly for the first time, from which he prepared his great book *Passion*,

brought out in 1939 by Ambroise Vollard with seventeen color etchings and eighty-two black-and-white wood engravings.

A number of critics have remarked on the similarity between Rouault's paintings and stained glass, and on his closer kinship to the religious artists of the twelfth or thirteenth century than to those of his own time. "My real life," Rouault said, "is back in the age of the cathedrals." It was an acute self-estimate. Perhaps the fact that in his youth he was apprenticed to a stained-glass maker had something to do in Rouault's later years with his matching of glowing, glasslike colors and his use of heavy, "leaded" outlines. Rouault did, however, study at the Ecole des Beaux-Arts under Gustave Moreau, whose foremost pupil he became and whose memory he was always, despite the contrasts between them, to revere. Moreau was a late romantic who luxuriated in exactly the profusion of detail that Rouault was to reject, and to whom religion was a useful source of mystery and inspiration rather than, as it became for Rouault, virtually the summing up of human experience and emotion.

Rouault's "descent into ugliness" was an escape from his dilemmas. He had to come out from the shadow cast by Moreau, and cast from behind Moreau by the towering Rembrandt; and at the same time he had to invent a vocabulary of belief in an unbelieving age. Even a believer like Léon Bloy, who wanted every painting to end in a prayer, would have preferred him to paint undisturbing angels, but that was not to be Rouault's fate. First and last, for him the cen-

TEXT CONTINUED ON PAGE 57

48

CHRISTUS

FIRST SINNERS

THE PRAYER

TO GOLGOTHA

ECCE DOLOR

VERONICA'S VEIL

CRUCIFIXION

PIETA

TEXT CONTINUED FROM PAGE 48

tral concerns were sin and redemption, and on them his eye rested with the unwavering gaze of a characteristically French conviction—austere, Jansenist, almost cruel in its certainties. "He was familiar with anguish," writes Lionello Venturi, "but not with doubt." In his clowns he painted the grotesque made lovable; even into his fallen women and monstrous judges he painted a certain natural grandeur; and always, as from his earliest days, he painted the sacred subjects, until the ones he returned to again and again, like the Crucifixion, grew in force and monumentality beyond anything achieved in religious art for many years before him.

"In his scenes of the Passion . . ." writes Maritain, "the imprint of Christ's face on Veronica's veil, which Rouault never tires of depicting [see page 54], seems to mean for him the imprint of divine mercy on human art. . . . The image of the Crucifixion, the 'capital sign of Christianity,' has been freed by him from that academicism to which it seemed condemned for two centuries."

Passion was the occasion for some of Rouault's greatest work. The etchings for the book were made by the master printer Roger Lacourière, and the wood engravings, which interpreted Rouault's originals, were cut by Georges Aubert; but it is nonetheless apparent that no process of transfer to another medium could reduplicate the freshness and power, the cumulative delicacy and density of the colors overlaying one another, which Rouault brought to these first transcripts—reproduced in the preceding pages—from his own hand.

Rouault's close association with the publisher and art dealer Vollard dated from 1917, when the latter became his exclusive agent. Vollard's influence on the art of his time had already been enormous. A clerk in a small gallery, he had become a dealer himself in 1893, and through energy and astuteness had managed to handle most of the important artists of the day. He organized the first major Cézanne exhibit, which caused a great scandal, in 1895. He put on the first Picasso show, in 1901; the first Matisse show, in 1904. When Vollard took on Rouault, he did so with a will—installing the painter in a studio in his own house in Paris.

Vollard's support was an undoubted asset to Rouault, but it was also a distraction; for Vollard had a consuming ambition to become the world's greatest publisher of fine prints and illustrated books, and to this end he drew heavily on Rouault's time and talent as a graphic artist. During the 1920's Rouault was in fact so occupied with making prints for Vollard that he found little time for painting, and it was for his prints (exhibited in New York in 1938) that he first became famous in America. Vollard was a perfectionist, publication was slow, and the relationship of painter to publisher was tempestuous: Rouault described it as "a barbed-wire entanglement." But the results justified the effort. Vollard said of the limited edition of *Passion,* when it finally appeared, "No one has ever made such books, and no one ever will again."

Passion consists of Rouault's illustrations to a text by the poet and intellectual André Suarès. It does not, as is apparent from the paintings, follow strictly the Biblical narrative but is, rather, a set of impressionistic meditations and variations on the theme of the Crucifixion. It is written in the often obscure language of French devout but avant-garde literature, which is far closer to poetry than to prose.

For example, the painting called "First Sinners" (page 50) does not at first appear to be at all a part of the New Testament narrative. Two aged peasants, according to the text, have been approached by a wretched-looking tramp. He inquires of them why they are digging three graves, to which they reply that two are for them and the third, perhaps, for him. They say he has the smell of blood about him and the look of crime; he explains that his crime was being born and that his name is Cain. They tell him that they know this well; they have recognized him. Their names are Eve and Adam.

The paintings for *Passion* to be exhibited are fifty-four in number, executed on heavy rag paper with a luminescent blue-green mat around each. They come from the Vollard collection and will have their first public viewing at the Valley House Gallery in Dallas, Texas, in mid-November.

MUSEUM OF MODERN ART, N. Y.

André Suarès by Rouault

SOTHEBY'S

PHOTOGRAPHS BY JOHN CHILLINGWORTH

In an antechaml

Silver wine cups, Roman perfume bottles, African bronze—not to mention Ming porcelain and Chippendale chairs—whatever mankind has valued comes sooner or later to London's legendary dealers in the fine arts

By WILLIAM K. ZINSSER

Perhaps the most dazzling gift shared by the nine men and one woman who own and manage Sotheby & Co., the London auction firm that has jumped to fame and wealth lately with its spectacular sales of paintings, is the ability to know a valuable object when they see one—even if they have never seen such an object before.

Typical of their scholarship and intuition, and of the route by which most items reach the firm, was an incident that took place last winter. A man brought in a curious round instrument, only three inches in diameter, that he had found in a secondhand shop. It was immediately taken, as all incoming objects are, to the appropriate Sotheby expert—in this case, T. H. Clarke, who heads the department called "objects of art."

Unlike the tidy realms that his colleagues supervise, such as silver or furniture or books, "objects of art" is a vague domain bounded on all sides by avid collectors and filled with strange and wonderful things: icons and miniatures, snuffboxes and glass paperweights, clocks and rings and, as Clarke puts it, "everything that isn't everything else." He so expects the unexpected to turn up on his desk every morning that he is never surprised when it does.

Still, the instrument that turned up on this particular morning was more than ordinarily unexpected, for nothing of its type had previously appeared. (Sotheby directors also seem to have total recall.) From its Islamic metalwork and Arabic script Clarke dated it to the Middle Ages and suspected its importance. To identify it more exactly he telephoned a science scholar and described the odd little globe.

"What you are describing," the scholar said, "is a spherical astrolabe, but I must warn you that it doesn't exist. We know from medieval manuscripts that it *did* exist, but nobody has ever found one." Obviously, however, somebody had found one. The unique object, lost for five hundred years and still guarding the secret of how it got to London, became the central jewel in an auction of instruments that Clarke was arranging, where it attracted lively interest and "fetched" $10,000.

To think of Sotheby's in these terms—as a game that any amateur can play—does not occur to a reader of newspapers. Judging by the glamourous auctions that the company holds so often and with such fanfare, it would seem to be a business only for art dealers and millionaires. Since last October it has had the largest single season ever of any fine-art auction house—

$22 million's worth, including the painting collections of Sir Alexander Korda and W. Somerset Maugham.

Yet the firm's success actually rests on the hundreds of smaller sales that it holds all year long, day in and day out. Its annual gross is now roughly $30,000,000—more than the combined income of its three principal rivals, Christie's of London, Parke-Bernet of New York, and the Galerie Charpentier of Paris—but this money does not come mainly from paintings or from a rich clientele. Two thousand people a day wander through the Sotheby building on New Bond Street; half the objects that they buy there cost less than $75, and only a small proportion of them are paintings.

It is this perpetual traffic with all sorts of people and all sorts of possessions that makes Sotheby's such a lively market place—and one so rich in surprises. No week elapses that somebody does not discover in his home an unremembered and unloved object whose value has risen to thousands of dollars. Generally he has no idea how steep the rise has been, and has been using his uncommon trophy for the commonest purpose. Last fall, after a Benin bronze was auctioned at Sotheby's for almost $8,000, two more of these extremely rare Nigerian heads were brought in by owners who saw newspaper accounts of the sale. One head had long served as a doorstop; the other had been repeatedly polished to a shiny yellow, like any household trinket, and so had lost all of its patina and much of its value. Nevertheless such events always stir a double sense of adventure at Sotheby's. The collector is thrilled by the appearance of a rarity that was not known to exist, and the seller is equally thrilled by the sum that the unwanted heirloom brings. It is one modern equivalent to finding buried treasure.

With such a vast daily turnover Sotheby's has become more than just a market place. It is a business giant which exerts power in many directions. The financial community watches it as an index to the economy; artists, designers, and dealers watch it as a weather vane that tells where the winds of taste are blowing. Almost nowhere are new currents so quickly felt. The objects that Sotheby's handles, after all, represent five thousand years of man's efforts to create beauty and every bizarre turn that his mind has taken in this pursuit. Thus the firm is in a position to satisfy the most finicky customer.

For the mind of the collector has been, if anything, even more bizarre than that of the artist. This strange bird, so given

At Sotheby's main auction room, an art dealer leans dangerously over a George III Carleton House desk to take a closer look at a Venetian canalscape

A Sotheby's man (left) hesitates over a bronze head of Voltaire before gently advising the owner it has little value

to unpredictable swoops, is the real center of the auction business, and the story of Sotheby's is largely the story of its ability to cater to the bird's fickle appetites. Who would expect anyone to pay, as a collector recently did, $3,500 for a glass paperweight of a snake swallowing a fly? Or $92,000 for a Louis XV commode?

In this story there is as much for the social historian as for the art historian to ponder. For never have so many people in so many countries been on such an art-buying spree, and never has the urge been so intertwined with factors that have nothing to do with art. Many of these factors are economic (art is a good investment and a tax benefit). Many are rooted in snobbery (art is the new status symbol). Some have their origin in modern architecture (people who live in glass houses can't have Grand Rapids furniture and *September Morn*). Some can be traced to that canny puppeteer, the interior decorator, who decrees from season to season which King George is in (III) and which is out (IV).

But whatever the motives, the result is the same. Art and antique prices continue their upward arc, and Sotheby directors see no end to the curve since the number of collectors is multiplying and the number of fine objects is not. In fact, it is shrinking. For dozens of new museums are being born, especially in the United States, and each must have its Picasso, its Queen Anne silver, Chippendale chair, Ming vase, and Egyptian head. When these objects lodge in a museum, they go out of circulation, and the remaining objects in individual homes become that much rarer. Privately the directors of

Sotheby's say that the current prices are "fantastic" and "ridiculous." But there is nothing ridiculous about their position as middlemen in the art stampede.

For a business so centrally fixed, Sotheby's is easy to miss on a stroll up New Bond Street. The old three-story building tends to disappear amid the other gilded shops, possibly because its façade is bisected by a newsstand. Like many English houses of a certain age, it derives part of its charm from not being entirely plumb. Perhaps it has been tilted by the hordes of pilgrims who swarm in every morning in search of a bargain, a good browse, or simply an entertaining show.

The show begins—in fact, the whole operation begins—downstairs at the counter where people bring the objects that they want to put up for auction. To watch this parade of odd-shaped bundles is to see how deeply the magpie instinct has taken hold in the human race. Old ladies rummage about in bulky reticules and fish out silver tea services. A Mayfair lady will stride in bearing a half-dozen sconces; another will be followed by her chauffeur carrying a mosaic table-top. Bearded Bohemians arrive with abstract paintings, bookish men with first editions and musty prints, dowagers with rolled-up rugs and Oriental pillows, and soon the counter is piled as high as a stall in an Arab bazaar, the objects having no common thread except that they are no longer wanted at home.

The girls behind the counter, increasingly harried as the morning races on, take the objects to a Sotheby director, or call one out to meet the object and its owner. This process is rather

This is a London dealer's last chance to inspect a precious antique Chinese porcelain: in a few moments it will be coming up for auction

like a doctor's examination: the object is poked and inspected while its parent stands nervously by. Frequently the verdict is disappointing:

"I'm afraid it *isn't* Queen Anne, Madam—much nearer Queen Victoria, unfortunately."

"It really isn't rare at all, Sir, I'm sorry to say, no matter what your grandmother told you. I doubt it would fetch three pounds."

"I must tell you that it isn't genuine. Mind you, it's a very *clever* fake, but we've seen several of these lately."

Back go the objects into the reticules and brown paper bags, unworthy of auction. If the verdict is favorable—that is, if the object has a certain market value—Sotheby's will estimate what it will fetch, and the owner will name a "reserve" price below which the auctioneer must not sell. So giddy is to-day's market, spurting up visibly from month to month, that these estimates can be far off. Not long ago a lady from Australia brought in a small James I wine cup (c. 1607) that she had never thought much of—she kept her car keys in it. The Sotheby man, struck by its grace and lineage, felt that it might fetch $2,000. The lady, eager to be rid of it, fixed the reserve at $900; the cup actually went for $3,400.

"It even surprised us," one director said, "and we're supposed to be experts." This phrase is heard often in Sotheby's nowadays, proving that the auction business is a game of chance that the auctioneer himself can never wholly control. He has no way of knowing who will turn up at an auction or what instructions bring them there. He cannot foresee the

whims and passions that goad two collectors to bid against each other, long after cooler heads have quit the field, for an object that only one of them can have. Nor can he predict the occasional moment when this process reverses itself, unaccountably, and all bidding stops far below the expected figure.

Every auction begins, in a sense, several weeks in advance, when a catalogue is mailed out to subscribers all over the world. In this deceptively simple booklet they can read an account of each item and decide whether to bid and how—in person, by mail, or through a dealer. (Auction firms tend to rise or fall on the reliability of their catalogues; the Sotheby staff prides itself on the careful scholarship of its books.) The customer's decision often hinges on how he deciphers the catalogue's special codes, particularly the one whereby Sotheby's declares a work to be authentic, possibly authentic, or probably not. The key to this code is the fullness of the artist's name. Thus a painting by "Sir Anthony Van Dyck" is genuine (one of these went last spring for $11,200), and a painting by "A. Van Dyck" is dubious (one of these went at the same auction for $785). Any further bobbing of the name would suggest that V. Dyck almost surely did not get anywhere near the canvas.

The auction itself is, of course, the main event of any day at Sotheby's. One is held every morning from eleven to one in the large green gallery on the second floor, and very often a book auction proceeds simultaneously in an adjoining room that is suitably dim and lined to the ceiling with books. The selling of books was the chief business of Sotheby's from its

Fred Rose, a Sotheby's director, takes the dais to preside over a sale of rare silver, including this George II Irish two-handled cup and cover

founding in 1744 until well into the twentieth century, when the art boom gathered momentum, and the ritual appears to have changed little in the two hundred-odd years since. Several dozen book dealers sit gravely in a circle beneath the auctioneer, who nods from side to side to accept their barely perceptible bids. This is an arena for experts: knowledge is precise, emotions are neat, and long tradition lends its august presence.

By contrast, the main gallery is a carnival where any fool can try his luck. At first it fills the visitor with awe. In the spiraling zeros of the auctioneer's voice—"two thousand pounds, two thousand five *hun*dred, *three* thousand pounds" —the private wealth of modern man seems limitless and overwhelming. But after several visits the room assumes its proper size and loses its goblins. The people are seen to be merely people, the objects shed their sanctity and are seen to be merely beautiful objects that anybody might have inherited or might aspire to buy. Often, in fact, they seem to be going at such a bargain rate that the visitor is tempted to jump into the bidding himself. Meanwhile he tries hard to keep his hand from wandering, frozen by the ancient fear that if he scratches his head he will acquire a Renoir. This danger is overestimated. Auctioneers can tell when a lady is bidding and when she is waving to a friend, even if the friend can't, and if in doubt they will ask.

Of the hundreds of people who attend every auction, relatively few are obvious dealers. They sit at a green baize table in front of the auctioneer with casual authority verging on boredom. The rest of the spectators drift in and out while the auction is in progress, greeting their friends, chatting, making notes, listening with half an ear, watching with half an eye and, at sporadic moments, wagging their catalogue to bid. So informal is the coming and going that the affair is very much like a large cocktail party. Presumably many Londoners make a habit of dropping in, during their morning rounds, to keep in touch with the market and with each other.

As a crowd they do not have, as might be expected, a common gold link. The aristocracy turns up in sufficient number to prove that the monocle, the eye-level bowler, the walking stick, and the tea-stained mustache are not figments of *Punch* cartoonists and English film makers. But the Mayfair set has no majority in the saleroom. Disheveled young artists, looking quite penniless, will suddenly bid on a painting—perhaps an earlier work of their own or of a still "undiscovered" friend. Mothers will stop in for a while with young children to give them a taste of beauty. Old men who have been attending auctions for fifty years will sit and exchange saleroom gossip until the one obscure item that interests them—antique firearms, possibly, or horse trappings—comes up for sale. American collectors, over on the night plane to get a specific object, will buy it and leave to catch the afternoon flight back. Sleek dealers from the Continent, in pinched suits and pointed shoes, buying for the "*Dolce Vita*" crowd at home, mingle the languages of Italy, France, Germany, and other lands into the

English brew—proof of how widely the items assembled for this auction will soon be scattered again.

The objects themselves are not, as in many auction houses, kept aloof from the customers and brought out at the moment of sale to be displayed from a stage. On the contrary, a visitor at an auction today may well sit on a Hepplewhite four-poster or stand on a valuable rug that will be sold out from under him that very morning. The glittering chandeliers overhead and the Flemish tapestries on the walls, which seem to be part of the permanent décor on Monday, will be gone by Friday and replaced by something else.

A similar hodgepodge fills the three small surrounding rooms, and browsers spend many hours there fondling silver, examining porcelain, and riffling through prints. A ladder is available for those who want an intimate look at the paintings, and it is not uncommon to see an old gentleman, beyond the age of exercise by ordinary standards, lug the ladder from one room to another, climb up it and peer at an old master, or pseudo old master, through a magnifying glass.

In this atmosphere of calculated clutter—Sotheby's has turned to picturesque advantage the fact that its building is too small—a visitor is beguiled into thinking that the ill-assorted objects will never be sorted out again. Beneath its quaint veneer, however, the firm rests on a solid base of artistic knowledge, business shrewdness, and human intuition.

For these three traits to exist in equal balance in one company is rare enough. That they should exist in one man is rarer still, and as this man is chairman of Sotheby's, he represents the ideal conjunction of man and job. In his eight years as boss, Peter Wilson has tripled the company's business and has been the chief architect of its rise. Now fifty, he bestrides the world art market like a colossus, or, more properly, like a sphinx, for in his cherubic face there is always the half-smile that hints at happy endings for everybody, at beautiful mysteries that only he can translate.

This mixture of charm and self-assurance has also become, by reflection, the personality of Sotheby's as a whole. "Before the war," says Wilson, who joined the firm at twenty-four and became a director at twenty-six, "the atmosphere was quite formal. I've tried to make it more easygoing. I want people to feel at home, whether they're here for any serious purpose or not. If you threw out 90 per cent of the visitors because they didn't come to bid, the sale would go less well. They contribute to the atmosphere."

Wilson's own personality is most potently on display when he "takes a sale." A very tall, blue-eyed man, whose accent purrs with the cadences of Eton, Oxford, and all else that is Established in the British order, whose striped pants and morning coat evoke the highest spheres of diplomacy, he looms out of the auctioneer's pulpit like a benign prime minister who has never lost a vote of confidence—and never expects to.

His voice can register shades of meaning so subtle that the human ear barely catches them. When he says, after the bid-

ngraved with armorials and a grinning satyr's face, later purchased for $728

Attentive buyers in the main auction room weigh their bids; to their right are stacked some of the canvases (by Augustus John and Philip Wilson Steer, among other British artists) that will go under the gavel.

ing about it. He recalls the moment with vast amusement. "It was absolutely idiotic," he says, giggling with delight.

Since then Wilson has captured many other brilliant auctions for Sotheby's—he has a way of turning up in Pittsburgh, say, or Milan, just when a collector is "ready to talk," and he would be a hard man *not* to entrust with a sale. His charm is one of the firm's most negotiable assets, and it is reinforced by an aesthetic judgment and commercial sense that his colleagues regard as infallible. Today the big auctions that he conducts are social events of the London scene—a fact demonstrated almost too well by the Maugham sale last April 9.

Into the protesting old building, at 9:30 P.M., pushed 2,500 people, or roughly a thousand more than could comfortably fit, and hundreds more were turned away. A large number were titled, moneyed, or vested with power; the remainder were vested with curiosity. A long platform sagged under newsreel and television cameras, which whirred so noisily that they often drowned out the bidders. Roving photographers shoved through the elegant crowd to snap such arriving mandarins as Lord Beaverbrook, and a nurse waited with great solemnity to revive the faint.

Under all this bodily pressure the renowned English calm buckled. Spectators jostled for position and took their losses badly. "Thank God at least we're in England," one old gentleman said, "and not in Italy: a charming people but very excitable." Those who couldn't squeeze into the main gallery were hurled back into various surrounding rooms, where they watched the auction on television and had their bids relayed by phone to the auctioneer. This, needless to say, was Peter Wilson, collating the different bids and tranquilizing the nervous throng. Within an hour he disposed of Maugham's thirty-five unexceptional paintings for almost $1,500,000, the highest price being $224,000 for a two-sided work by Picasso, and retired secure in the knowledge that the sale would make the front page of the New York *Times* the next day.

The firm would also be richer by $150,000. Its standard commission is 10 per cent, or considerably less than that of its competitors in other countries, such as Parke-Bernet, which charge 12 to 22 per cent. As a result, countless Americans now send their objects abroad for auction at Sotheby's. Since these objects are frequently bought by other Americans, it is common for paintings to cross the ocean, change ownership, and take one of the next boats back. Several other economic factors also conspire in the firm's favor. One was a decision of the British Treasury in 1954 to ease restrictions on importing works of art from the United States and to let sellers be paid in the currency of their own country. There is also the fact that Sotheby's will not reveal who sold an object if the seller does not want his name known.

The visible drama of the Sotheby auction room is produced by much invisible machinery, run by nine partners in addition to Wilson, who share the profits and pleasures of the business. Each is an expert in one field and often in many more—for

ding has soared to a vast sum and suddenly come to a halt, "three thousand pounds, then," or "three thousand only," there is just enough extra weight on "then" or "only" to convey a tinge of disappointment, almost of disbelief, that an object of such value should be going for so little. Often this nudges the bidders back into action and they drive the price up still higher.

Wilson's most shameless performance took place four years ago at the Jakob Goldschmidt auction, where seven impressionist paintings went for $2,186,800. This was the first of the fabulous auctions of the postwar era and the one that announced the arrival of Sotheby's at the top of the heap. So huge were the prices, by 1958 standards, as the sale proceeded —a Van Gogh fetched $369,000, a Manet $316,400—that the spectators were tense when Cézanne's *Boy in a Red Waistcoat* came up. Bidding soon reached the unprecedented figure of $616,000 and then paused. In the ensuing silence Wilson said: "Will nobody bid any more?" The outrageous remark, so casually delivered, broke the room into laughter and broke the tension for good. Nobody *did* bid any more, and Wilson is not sure to this day that he didn't abridge the sale. If so, he isn't worry-

example, J. C. Butterwick is an authority on books and silver, and A. J. B. Kiddell, a specialist in porcelain, is consulted on almost any baffling object that strays into the house.

In this respect, and because each man runs his own department independently, Sotheby's resembles a small college, whose professors are bound in a fellowship of learning and taste. They work hard, at tasks that are essentially academic: selecting, evaluating, and cataloguing the objects that they will subsequently auction, and at the same time teaching their junior assistants ("What's the one thing wrong with that vase?"). They occupy cramped offices, which can hardly be reached because the aisles are clogged with objects awaiting auction, and they sit at desks littered with treasures awaiting their scrutiny. Their phones ring and their doors open constantly to admit some question that needs an immediate answer or to inform them that they must fly to Madrid right away to appraise a collection. Sometimes an assistant or secretary will come in and rummage through their desk drawers to find —or not to find— a momentarily misplaced object. Harried by detail, they still —like professors—do not regard what they do as work. It is a game that never fails to divert.

"We just sit here like Micawber waiting for things to turn up," says R. S. Timewell, head of the furniture department. "Recently an old lady near Cambridge wrote that she wanted to raise $5,500 and asked if I would go through her house and see if her furniture would fetch that much. I did, and one room turned out to have a very fine eighteenth-century chest that the old lady was using to store blankets in. 'Your worries are over,' I told her, 'if you sell that chest.' She said, 'But that's quite impossible—where will I store my blankets?' I told her that she could buy a new chest for about $25 and store her blankets in that. She said, 'That sounds a good idea.' The chest was auctioned for $6,500 and is now a prize piece in an American home."

Sometimes this happens on a scale so big as to sound like romantic fiction. "Several years ago a Captain Berkeley wrote us," recalls Frederick Rose, director of the silver department, "and said that he had a silver dinner service for which someone had offered him $140,000, and he wondered if he should accept the offer. I didn't know of this particular service, nor, it seems, did anybody else. I went out to Berkeley Castle to see it, and it turned out to be a 168-piece Louis XV service by Jacques Roettiers, one of only three to survive the French Revolution.

"I felt that it would fetch a much higher price if it were put up to public competition. On the day of the auction Captain Berkeley came and said he hoped we had made the right decision. Well, the opening bid was $140,000—from the same man who had made the original offer—and after that the bidding went up in multiples of five thousand pounds. It was all over in two minutes: the service sold for $579,600. And Captain Berkeley only had it insured for $8,000."

It may seem inconceivable that such a treasure could remain a secret in a nation where almost nothing has gone un-

A dramatic moment on the other side of the auction room: a woman signals her offer to Sotheby's chairman, who is conducting the proceedings; a sideboard, lower right, serves as one buyer's hat stand.

recorded since 1066. Yet the great houses of England are only beginning to yield their ancestral treasures. This is especially true of paintings, according to Carmen Gronau, the firm's expert on old masters and its only woman director. "There's an enormous fund of pictures in England," says Mrs. Gronau, "that is unlike anything else in the world.

"The wealth of this country came in the eighteenth and nineteenth centuries, when the sons went on the Grand Tour and bought paintings. The large collections are all known, but the bread and butter comes from the broad general fund, from what the trade calls 'a good country source,' which is something that comes fresh on the market. The owners of these works have always just had them on the wall and taken them for granted—until now. When Franz Hals's *Portrait of a Cavalier* came to us for auction two years ago—it sold for $509,000—it was almost completely unknown. It had only been exhibited once, in 1922, in a provincial museum."

Equally hidden from the public all these years was Rembrandt's *Saint Bartholomew*, which Major Kincaid Lennox sold several months ago at Sotheby's for $532,000 to J. Paul

Getty. Major Lennox seldom admits people who want to see his inherited collection, which includes two other Rembrandts and a Van Dyck, and which shares a room in his Shropshire castle with a television set and a parakeet; but in due time these masterpieces should also emerge into public view.

It is the need for money, after all—especially money to meet huge death duties and other taxes—that is dislodging the great hoards of art, silver, furniture, jewelry, and books from the stately homes of Albion. Those who listen closely at Sotheby's hear more than the crack of the auctioneer's gavel. They hear the cracking of ancient estates, the tottering of peerages and, in the distance, the onrush of the new rich—Englishmen who made postwar fortunes in scrap or realty, Greek shipping magnates, Italian and German industrialists, American oil tycoons, all of them eager for the attributes of status and taste that can be had at Sotheby's for the raising of a hand and the writing of a check.

"The demand for fine objects is so great," says Mr. Timewell, "that people will buy almost anything, regardless of whether it's in fashion. Not Americans, though. When a style goes out of vogue in the United States, nobody there will buy it. I gather that tapestries, for example, are unsalable in America today. But Italian, Dutch, German, and English buyers are very keen on them."

The tapestries are proof of the fact that in today's art market almost nothing is a dud. Every department head at Sotheby's, surveying his field, bears this out. In silver, for instance, it is generally assumed that "you can double or even triple your money in five years." According to Mr. Rose, "teapots of George II and later are the only things I'm not particularly keen to see come in at the moment."

"All fine books have appreciated in value," says A. R. A. Hobson, head of the book department, "and medieval manuscripts also keep rising. In 1900 Sotheby's sold an eleventh-century manuscript of Boethius for $100; a few years ago it came through again and fetched $18,000." In 1960 Hobson concluded an auction of manuscripts collected by C. W. Dyson Perrins which brought almost $2,500,000. He has also presided over the gradual sale of three private libraries—libraries so big that they took eight, ten, and sixteen years, respectively, to auction off. Annual sales of books at Sotheby's now total roughly $3,000,000.

In antique furniture only two styles, according to Mr. Timewell, are "relatively out of vogue: very elaborately carved furniture of about 1800, and Renaissance furniture, which was tremendously high at the turn of this century." Modern art is booming—and breeding a new race of British art lovers, according to R. J. Rickett, the firm's expert on everything less old than an old master. "Up to now," he says, "hunting, shooting, and fishing have been the occupational pastimes in England, and the pictures on English walls were faded aquatints of Midlands steeplechases. Anyone who collected modern art was considered Bohemian or a very queer fellow."

"There are nowhere near enough early Chinese ceramics to go around," Kiddell, Sotheby's porcelain expert, points out. "The keenest demand is for blue and white wares of the Yuan and early Ming period. I remember several years ago a teenage boy came in with a fifteenth-century blue and white dish. He had bought it in a junk shop in the East End for $15 because he thought it looked valuable, and it was—it sold for $7,000. It can still be done if you're alert, but it's getting harder. Books are beginning to raise the general level of awareness."

This is a point that all the Sotheby directors make in accounting for the boom in their business. Art books, films, museums, and other media have spread art knowledge on a broad popular base, and even the most esoteric fields are no longer the province of the scholarly few. Inevitably this has increased the desire to own fine objects and is driving collectors to find new fields. Their restless search is felt at Sotheby's mainly in the antiquities department.

By now, of course, the great antiquities have been put into museums and out of reach. Quite a few countries have also adopted stern rules—notably Egypt, Greece, Italy, India, and Nigeria—to keep their national treasures from leaving the country. Yet certain unusual art forms keep turning up to pique the collector's fancy. One is "Roman glass," a name given to the iridescent vials and scent bottles of the Roman Empire. These objects have jumped into popular demand in the past few years. So have pre-Columbian gold ornaments, Etruscan statues, and Cycladic Greek figures. Haida objects are also catching on: these are small bone and ivory carvings of the Haida tribe in British Columbia.

"Of course nobody really knows," says Mr. Clarke, speaking of the whole inflated market, "what any of the objects that come up for auction today are worth. If they did, there wouldn't be any auction business."

"You must deal with every sale as a special problem, not by an established system," says Peter Wilson. "It is an art, not a science." Under his leadership Sotheby's has learned to practice this art with near-scientific precision. Yet he knows that the current boom can be explained only up to a point in terms of snobbery, tax laws, investments, publicity, education, and other such factors. Far more subtle forces are at work which unbalance the formula, adding new elements of mystery and surprise.

"For many people," Wilson says, "buying a fine object is buying a stake in the future. It takes the place of religion, especially in insecure times. It's like old people planting trees. A gentleman of eighty thinks nothing of planting a forest of trees. After the war, the first items to rise dramatically in price were porcelains, the most fragile of all. If you buy a very fragile object, or a very rare or beautiful object, you are saying that life is going to go on."

William K. Zinsser, a free-lance writer and frequent contributor to Horizon, *wrote "Encode Me, My Sweet Encodable You" for the September, 1962, issue.*

In Sotheby's storage rooms an endle

cession of treasures comes briefly to rest before going on sale. The lonely lady with uplifted arm is not a statue but one of a pair of candelabras

On Stage: MATT TURNEY

In the traditional—that is, classical—dance, grace results from a harmony between the dancer's spiritual intention and physical achievement. But the performance of modern dance comes from almost the opposite source: a personal excitement, an almost religious struggle between a purity of spirit and the awkwardness of the body. It is this struggle that creates the tensions that make the modern dance "modern," and not ballet. These tensions are evident in the long, sweeping, quick-limbed motions of Matt Turney, the young dancer who, since her first triumph in 1954, has ranged from Lilith to Lightning as a soloist with Martha Graham's company. After every lithe, soul-searching movement, Miss Turney leaves behind severe doubts as to which—the divine or the awkward—really *is* the purer element.

The problem is that body of hers—"five-foot, eight-and-a-half, *maybe* nine." It is so commanding physically that it is like a divining vertical stroke down the center of any dance ensemble. One critic has described her as "a goddess in every slender inch of her body." Whenever she moves—slowly or suddenly, but always with that awesome reach—she seems to dramatize a conflict between heaven and earth. Even her hands suffer the same fate. They are long, slender, exquisitely expressive. Yet clasped in a simple dancer's prayer, they seem to draw all her lines up too powerfully into one mighty angle. Or stretched above her head, like brown pods that have just broken open, they find their own release from the tensions of her dance. What she says in admiration of her most influential teacher, Miss Graham—"Martha's mind works according to no natural laws"—really applies even more to herself: her *body* seems to work according to no natural laws.

"I know how I like to move," she explains. "I like to know absolutely rhythmically what I'm doing. Then I like to move through space rather than to do the small, precise thing. I guess Lightning would be about right."

Lightning is one of her more felicitous roles in a new dance called *A Look at Lightning,* created by Miss Graham just this past season. Three lethargic, graceless male dancers look at Miss Turney. In her they see the prophetess, and are directly touched by the revelation. This clairvoyant guise is common to most of her portrayals: even back in 1951, in her first major appearance with the Graham Company, she rose up chthonically as She of the Earth in *Dark Meadow.* True, she has come down from prophecy occasionally to create such baggage as Lilith in *Embattled Garden*—stretching out lime green in the sun, cooling herself with an orange fan— but her more accustomed atmosphere is a spiritual remoteness. Significantly, among all the roles that Miss Graham has abstracted from the figure of Saint Joan for her master-work of dance hagiology, *Seraphic Dialogue,* the Martyr is the one she assigned Miss Turney.

Her success in 1954 in the role of The Pioneer Woman was sudden, but she was "eager and ready" for it. She has had "the performing bug" ever since junior high school, back in Milwaukee, when a dancing teacher named Nancy McKnight suggested how she might channel all her athletic energies. She went to the University of Wisconsin and studied under Margaret H'Doubler as a dance major, danced jazz routines around the university—"the lawyers' ball, that kind of thing" —and became one of six dancers in a summertime venture called the Wisconsin Dance Group, all of whom piled into an old Chevrolet, barnstormed the country, and performed wherever they could find enough candlelight.

Out of two dancing summers—which took them through the U.S.A. and into Canada, setting up their candles in one dining hall after another—came "certain people who were just destined to be with each other." Three of the six eventually came to the Graham School in New York, making their debut together in *Canticle for Innocent Comedians,* and Mary Hinkson, now Miss Turney's fellow soloist with the Graham Company, is still one of her closest friends.

At the moment Miss Turney, living on Park Row, is in a more or less relaxed mood: her only commitments are a nightly performance in the Broadway musical *Milk and Honey* and "a husband and a dog to take care of." Her husband is Robert Teague, a sports writer for the New York *Times,* whom she met and married in 1957, having somehow missed him both in Milwaukee and at the University of Wisconsin. The dog is her excuse to take walks during which she secretly practices.

"You keep trying to find the perfect 'alignment.' Sometimes you do it just walking down the street," she admits. The alignment is that elusive requirement of the modern dance, which depends so much on the body's moment of poise—and to achieve it she is even willing to risk what purists of the modern dance would consider traffick with the devil, an occasional ballet lesson.

Actually this helps her follow "unscientific, terribly personal" devices of her own, all aimed at bringing the body into the graceful, working alignment. "I have to keep telling myself, 'Don't lose that connection between the hips and the legs,'" she said during an interview in her apartment. "Because if I do lose it, I can't make the double turn."

In fact, with a slightly worried expression, she got up and did a double turn, just to be sure. She looked a little stiff and double-turned again—*that* way, it seemed—and sat down comfortably once more, without a knot in her whole long body.

BROCK BROWER

Photograph by JERRY BA

church with a twist

A Connecticut parish has defied the traditions of New England architecture and built a

From the eastern seabord to the Pacific, America today is the scene of an eruption in church building remarkable in scope and surprising in looks. Architecturally, the service of God in this country is now more adventurous than that of Mammon or other worldly interests. Nothing in our new glass-box banks and offices or in our stripped-down and scrupulously functional schools and houses can approach the free-form exuberance of our latest churches, particularly in the suburban wildwood, where they take on such shapes as a whale, a teepee, or a saucer. It is as if churchgoers were now out en masse to mock tradition (including that most rigid of traditions, functionalism), and as if the sanctuary had become the last play area of American architecture.

Take the instance of the startling, conical edifice just com-

pleted by the United Church of Rowayton, Connecticut, a prosperous exurb forty miles outside of New York City. Every community and congregation faced with growth and change confronts its individual debate over what kind of a church to build.

The debate at Rowayton reached a height of controversy that threatened to split the town as well as the congregation—a group of some eighty families of several denominations who had come together, or "united," for the purpose of common worship. Yet, although the proposed new church was denounced by some as "the Rowayton twist" and worse, its sponsors prevailed, and the United Church remains united under the upswept rafters of a creation the ages may overlook but its neighbors cannot.

It spirals above the primly gabled roofs of the town's com-

The irregular conical peak (far left) of the new United Church of Rowayton, Connecticut, looms over the squat, conventional shape of the same congregation's Meeting House. With its free-form design and curvilinear roof (center), the church points outward and upward, its central element rising to a swirling spire partially enclosed by glass. The ribbed interior and concrete pulpit are inspected (above) by the pastor, Rev. Donald Emig, and the architect, Joseph Salerno of Westport, Connecticut.

house of worship uniting modern design with timeless reverence By RUSSELL BOURNE

fortable houses with the shaggy eccentricity of a physics professor at a liberal arts school. It stands on the same corner lot as a fifty-year-old Baptist church (from which many of its members came), like a shrine of a wholly different, more casual sort of religion. And it symbolizes the trend of church building in this country's tradition-bound, God-fearing communities: incongruous, sensational, sometimes profoundly dedicated.

The Rowayton "House of Worship," as its parishioners call it, was not the first building to be erected by the United Church. Out in the back of the lot is the Meeting House the congregation put up in 1954. It is modern and functional in plan and mass, but the exterior has been finished with traditional brick and clapboard siding. This is precisely the indecisive, going-nowhere type of structure that one might fear

church people would build in an era that has been called post-Christian. "The only good thing about the Meeting House," says Robert Moore, a former member of the United Church's building committee, "is what we learned not to do again from it. We learned not to send out a survey to the community asking what everybody wanted. We learned not to trust an architect to know any more than he should about our business. And we learned that we really had to think through in detail what we were doing."

It appears from this that the House of Worship, for which plans were made six years later, in 1960, was not just a sculptor's whim. Subcommittees and yardsticks were as necessary as *élan*. The building committee itself was by then made up of eleven men and one woman representing twelve different parts

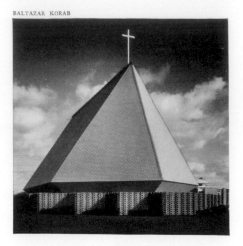

Three unorthodox American designs: from left to right, an Episcopal church for Burien, Washington; Methodist for Warren, Michigan, and Greek Orthodox for Wauwatosa, Wisconsin. The architects are Durham, Anderson & Freed; Minoru Yamasaki; and Frank Lloyd Wright.

of the consolidated congregation. All of them (but not the pastor and the architect, who also served on the committee) were required to pass through a philosophical needle's eye: they had to agree that they would approach the design of the House of Worship without predilections. This vow of intellectual chastity was necessary if only because Rowayton, like many another small suburban community, suffered something of a revolution after World War II; its population doubled (from 1,600 to 3,000), and violent things happened to its average age (down) and its average income (up). Neither its long-time residents nor its new arrivals, moreover, are persuaded that the revolution is over.

The Reverend Donald W. Emig, a Methodist, has been ministering to this mixed suburban flock for the past eleven years; he joined the building committee with understandable trepidation. "I had seen other congregations in nearby towns ripped apart by controversial structures," he says, "and I knew we had trouble ahead." Yet Emig is no compromiser, as the church built under his leadership attests. A short, ruddy man, given to pointing at things with the chewed end of his pipe, he pads about the new building with an air of astonishment. He marvels at what has happened to him and his church; he is ingenuously surprised at the world's goodness. But he knows that the world requires courage as well as good humor.

Soon after he came to Rowayton to be pastor of an old-line, faltering Methodist church, he found himself part of an effort to merge that church with the local Baptists. "The first phase," Emig recalls, "was that we'd meet one month in one church, the next month in the other. But soon everyone—or nearly everyone—realized the falseness of the separation."

Emig assumed that after the merger had been completed he would go on to another Methodist church elsewhere. But the responsible officials of the National Methodist Church viewed his activities in Rowayton with severe disfavor. "They didn't understand," Emig explains, "that what had to be done to minister to those postwar families from so many different parts of the country was something truly new. Or, to put it another way—the old life had to be lost that a new one might be found."

The churchmen went ahead with the joining of the churches, and Emig, undaunted, accepted the call to stay on in Ro-

wayton. He then urged his combined flock to ally themselves with the United Church of Christ (as Congregationalists are now called), which one might think would have destroyed Rowayton's chances of ever having a very exciting new church building. For the Congregationalists, despite their tradition of independence, have rarely wavered from a devotion to the architecture of centuries past. Emig believed it was nonetheless important for his new church to establish denominational ties with them so that its members would not "lose a voice in matters relating to nationwide Christian concern."

It was also Emig who urged the members of his church to take on the challenge of building a new sanctuary—not because the old, crenelated Baptist church was too small or could not be expanded, but because it seemed committed to a dead generation's forms and symbols and thus spiritually restrictive. And as the members of the building committee began the long, wearying business of interviewing architects who applied for the commission, they recognized that they were looking for something more than a space merchant. For this reason they rejected many prestigious and well-qualified church designers. "I remember the guy who kept asking us what we wanted," says committeeman Moore. "He'd built this kind of church here and that kind of church there; it was just a matter of what ready-made plans we wanted him to pull out of the drawer." After narrowing the number of applicants down from seventeen to four, by a slim margin the committee chose Joseph Salerno of nearby Westport, Connecticut, an independent architect with a diversified, if selective, practice.

Like Emig, Salerno has had opportunities to conform to the established patterns of suburbia—and has preferred to remain an individualist. He did indeed listen to the committee; he attended church services, church suppers, and church socials. But as the design began to take shape in his mind, his tolerance diminished. Moore expresses it this way: "We thought we were a good committee with some valid ideas; Joe Salerno picked up a lot of them but anything that didn't fit he threw out. We had the effect of pushing him—only in the direction he wanted to go." Significantly, Salerno's best-known church before Rowayton was a design for Weston, Connecticut, that was rejected because of its radicalism; he had not been interested in modifying it.

Given a studious and unprejudiced building committee, an independent-minded architect, and a blithe minister, it was perhaps to be expected that the initial proposal for the United Church's House of Worship did not conform to any recognizable example of New England church building. The only surprising thing was that the congregation—which included a group of middle-aged ladies who formed its Fidelis Club—eventually accepted it.

In the new building's design there is a haunting, internal echo of the old Baptist church. Both seating plans are semicircular. But the resemblance goes no further. In the creaking, "Akron-style" Baptist church, attention centers on one awkward corner; in the new building, it focuses on a simple altar above which rises a glowing cone of laminated wooden beams brightly washed with light admitted through colored glass panes. "The light coming down to the altar is an indication that God is with us," Salerno explains. "And the semicircular seating plan represents unity of the people. What has always worried me about traditional churches with one high element —the steeple—and one low—the nave—is that the two things really don't go together. I wanted one continuous, enveloping idea, and I think we got it in the twist of the spine."

Like most contemporary buildings, the Rowayton House of Worship started with a functional plan. Subcommittees of the building committee loaded the table with reports: on whether the choir should be in front or in back; how much room the Sunday School would require; and what provision should be made for special services. "But while the committee was struggling in two dimensions," Moore recalls, "Joe Salerno was thinking in three. He worked with tiny clay models, and one night he showed us in three models how his thinking had been developing. The first was squarish; that's where he'd started. And then they got rounder. The third one had this continuous roof line going up and not stopping—unity and eternity. We knew that related to us."

They also knew that considerable education would be necessary before the church's 425 active members shared the committee's architectural excitement. And they decided to apply the education in one massive dose. No word of the design was leaked to the congregation before the presentation meeting on the night of Palm Sunday, 1961. It was a well-attended gathering, and the committee was ready.

"When the first slide went on the screen, there was this kind of gasp," Emig is fond of relating, "and then silence, until the committee began the lecture, putting all of Joe's ideas into their own words. After that everyone wandered around the model of the building—it was wonderful. To my surprise, somebody introduced a motion that the proposal be accepted, and before anyone could say much of anything it was passed: 174 for proceeding into working drawings, 14 against."

Not everyone was convinced. With the indignation of women who have been asked to swallow a big, woolly, masculine concept, the Fidelis Club balked, as did some other conservative parishioners. The ladies of the club, who usually occupy themselves with activities to benefit the church, then dedicated themselves to the defeat of the proposed building. But they wanted to fight in specific terms—why can't we have a traditional New England church with a traditional spire?—not in terms of the architectural generalities the committee members had diligently learned and now used to defend their decision.

The deadline for the opposition to gather enough votes to defeat the proposal was the following November. But they found that, although they might pick up a few "con" votes here and there from the older residents, the "pro's" kept gaining among the newcomers. And most frustrating of all was the fact that the solid front of the committee could not be split open. "Only one committeeman was unenthusiastic about the design," Moore remembers, "but he had too much respect for the committee by then to want to oppose the majority and its proposal actively. So we felt confident enough, and of course obligated, to invite the Fidelis Club to come and tell us what they were upset about. For some reason they never showed up."

The opposition recognized the firm hold that the new building had on the imaginations of the congregation. When the final presentation was made, the vote was virtually the same as at the Palm Sunday meeting. But a vocal majority of the church members are deeply pleased with their nonconforming building.

The style and the shape of the House of Worship are indeed strangely suited to the mood of Rowayton churchgoers. Beneath their outward conservatism there is a level of gaiety, a maverick impatience that is not wholly new to American Protestantism. It shows through in more important ways than a sports car in the church parking lot or the percentage of twist records at a youth fellowship dance. It can be seen with all its contradictions in this statement prepared by the building committee when they were searching for an architect:

"We are a cosmopolitan people, liberal and free, by virtue of background and exposure to cosmopolitan influences. Some of us are residents of long standing with family traditions in this small Long Island Sound community. An increasingly greater number, however, are newer arrivals from all parts of the United States, with religious backgrounds that encompass all denominations of the Christian Church. Most of us own our own homes, have several children, commute to New York or surrounding cities, work hard on house and yard.

"We are generally not well-grounded by upbringing, experience, or training in formal religious doctrine and cultures. Many of the younger families among us were born in the materialistic period after World War I, with a resulting questioning of traditional religious expressions. This is the first church to which many of us have belonged. . . ."

There is, however, a freshly minted character to the Rowayton church that is something more than newness or unorthodoxy. The force of the winding roof line *does* draw you in; the concentric circles of the seating plan *do* draw you toward the altar. Not everyone, of course, is moved by the thrust of the eccentric spire and delighted by the bare wood of the interior as are these Christians in Rowayton. They face unconcernedly the possibility that their sanctuary will seem as imperfect to the next generation of worshipers as the old Baptist church does to them. They did not build their House of Worship as a beacon for the future or a monument to the past, but as a tent in which their souls might find first aid. Perhaps that is why their church looks momentarily so right.

Russell Bourne, formerly an associate editor of Architectural Forum, *is now editor of* HORIZON CARAVEL BOOKS.

IN PRINCI
PIO

ERAT UERBUM

UERBUM ERAT

APUD DM DX

Though holocausts, hatreds, and forgetfulness have obliterated vast treasures of past cultures, occasional good luck, later circumspection, and modern recovery have rescued a priceless part of our written legacy from oblivion

THE WONDROUS SURVIVAL OF RECORDS

An eloquent instance of the chances and mischances that surround the survival of precious records is given by the Lindisfarne Gospels (opposite), a book inscribed about A.D. 700 at a monastery on the northeast coast of England, lost at sea, and miraculously recovered. The illuminated manuscript, a rendering of the four Gospels, carries above its Latin lines a translation in the old Northumbrian dialect, making this the earliest "English" version of them in existence. The page shown here opens the Gospel of Saint John, reading (with its first three letters conjoined) IN PRINCIPIO ERAT VERBUM ET VERBUM ERAT APUD D[EU]M ET D[EU]S. *But, old as it is, the Lindisfarne book is young compared to the limestone tablet (right) found at Kish in Iraq. Dated c. 3500 B.C., this is the oldest example of picture writing yet discovered. Among its images are a head, hand, foot, and sledge.*

By GILBERT HIGHET

The other day I met a friend of mine, an author who is successful and ambitious. Asking him about his work, I found him profoundly depressed. In a few years, he said somberly, there won't be any books. They will all be destroyed, and there will be nobody left to read them. It is difficult to argue with anyone who thinks he foresees the end of civilization; but I tried to console him. Mankind has endeavored to kill itself off before this, and its books have nearly all been destroyed. Yet as long as there was someone who wanted to read, books and records have been saved.

Nevertheless, it still strikes me with amazement when I open a book of speeches by Demosthenes and begin to hear the voice, the very syllables and cadences, of a man who died some twenty-three centuries ago. Surely it is almost miraculous that we can take up the *Aeneid* of Vergil, printed by machinery that would have astonished Vergil himself, on a material he had never seen, in a format he could scarcely have imagined, and after two millennia find that, undimmed by time and change, his poetry still sings, his mystical visions still transport us as they did his first readers, and the subtleties of his poetic architecture still hold secrets only half-discovered.

The miracle of the preservation of thought through marks on a smooth surface is commemorated every week by one of the most impressive little religious ceremonies in the world. Every Sabbath in every Jewish synagogue, a handwritten copy of the Torah, the first five books of the Bible, is taken out of its palace. After a reading, the book is carried through the congregation before it is returned to the ark, and every pious Jew kisses it. It is always handwritten with a quill pen. It is always in the form of a parchment roll. Its text is always exactly the same as that of its predecessor, from which it was copied: the very letters are counted so that they may never vary by a jot, any more than the law of God Almighty can vary. By doing homage to the book in this way, the Jews express their devotion to the name of the Creator contained in the Torah; but they also, by implication, express reverence for one of man's greatest inventions—the written book.

The Jews, like the Moslems, have always carried their sacred writings with them: the book and the people have sustained each other. But among the Greek and Latin classics there are no such sacred books: the nations for whom they were written have disappeared; their very languages have assumed new shapes and sounds—remote, although not wholly different from the original tongues. How have the great books of the past survived through so many centuries?

First, we must sadly admit that many, very many, of them have been lost. In Greece and the Greek-speaking world, and later in the Roman world, there were many libraries and many hundreds of thousands of books. Literacy was more widespread in the second century of our era than it was in the eighteenth. The walls of Pompeii, covered with public announcements and private scribbles in three languages (Latin, Greek, and Oscan), show how natural and commonplace was the use of writing then. Nearly all townsfolk could read, freemen and slaves alike. Only on the farms and ranches were many people illiterate. In Egypt excavators now dig up large private book collections buried under the sand near villages where today few of the fellahin own a single book, or could read it if they did.

Although some authors of antiquity composed only a few works, to which they gave all their life's energy, there were many who produced an amazing number of them. The comedian Aristophanes left fifty-four plays. Aeschylus, first of the great tragic dramatists, wrote at least eighty. Livy's history of Rome ran into one hundred and forty-two volumes; and such polygraphs were not exceptional. But of many of the most famous authors we have only a few scanty though precious relics. It is as though we had the titles of all Shakespeare's plays, with some fragments quoted from most of them, but possessed complete only *Hamlet, Henry V, A Midsummer-Night's Dream,* and *As You Like It.* Of Aristophanes' half a hundred comedies, we have just eleven. Of Aeschylus's four score plays, only seven survive. We have a summary of virtually all of Livy's Roman history, so that we know what he covered in each volume, but only thirty-five of his one hundred and forty-two volumes remain. And while these great writers have survived in however meager a proportion, dozens of others have vanished almost without a trace. Aristophanes was only one of a large school of competing comic dramatists. From quotations and allusions, we know the names of about a hundred and seventy poets of the "Old Comedy" (the group to which Aristophanes belonged) with 1,483 titles of their plays. Except Aristophanes, not one survives. Where is his great rival, boozy old Cratinus? Where is the energetic Eupolis, whom Horace linked with the other two in a gay triad? Gone, except for a few jokes, some famous passages preserved in quotation, and many play titles. It is delightful to look through the titles and reflect how much fun the Athenians had in the fifth century before Christ; it is painful to remember how much of it has vanished.

But not all. It would scarcely be worth studying classical literature if it were a heap of insignificant debris. It is not. It is like a city which has been bombed and partially burned, so that whole sections are in ruins and some streets with their houses are irrecoverable; but at its heart many of the most important and beautiful public buildings stand unscathed, full of statues and pictures and memories, while others, although damaged, retain a noble tower or one magnificent wing. The two epics of Homer (or of the two Homers) are safe. All Vergil's poetry is intact. The works of Plato are complete and have even acquired some "Platonic" forgeries in the meantime. We have all that Horace ever published. We can read virtually all of Lucretius and Terence and Catullus in Latin, virtually all of Demosthenes

This antique double exposure is a page from one of the most famous of palimpsest ("rescraped") manuscripts. During the Dark Ages it was a common practice to scrape the writing from unread books and use the valuable parchment over again. But the ghost of the old text often lingered beneath the new, waiting to be discovered by the scholars of a later age (nowadays aided by chemicals and infrared photographs). In this case a fourth-century manuscript of Cicero's On the State *(double columns) was found to underlie a late seventh-century copy of a work by Saint Augustine. Until the Vatican librarian Angelo Mai recovered it from these pages in 1822, the Cicero was known only in fragmentary form.*

and Thucydides and Herodotus in Greek, and virtually all of a few other first-rate writers in either tongue. Furthermore, we have the complete works of a number of authors who, although not "classics" either in their own time or now, are amusing, shocking, informative, or creatively eccentric. We do not have too many of the classical books from Greece and Rome, but we have much of the best.

The great books of Greece and Rome were written down between 800 B.C. and A.D. 450. They were first printed and disseminated to many modern readers between A.D. 1450 and 1550. Once printed, they were likely to survive because they were so good or because there were now so many copies of them (duplication means preservation). But between the distant centuries when the classics were composed and the comparatively recent centuries when they were reproduced by the man with the machine, grave obstacles and recurrent perils often threatened to obliterate them.

First came the danger that haunts us all. Anyone born since 1900 has grown up with it always in his mind. It is the great destroyer, the waster, the terrible simplifier—war. It is always more violent than we expect. It is capricious. In the conflict of human wills, deliberation and choice and purposive action are often sacrificed to sheer destructive energy. When the Crusaders were sacking Constantinople in 1204, a drunken soldier was seen tearing up the sacred books of the Hagia Sophia.

King Matthias Corvinus of Hungary (1440–1490) had collected a magnificent library of manuscripts, some written for him by Italian calligraphers and some bought by his agents in Greece and Asia Minor (see cover and page 95). Part of it was captured by the Turks in 1541 during their advance into central Europe and some specimens were sent back to Istanbul. The others were left in storage, damaged by fire and carelessness, recaptured in 1688, and divided up among the conquerors. And yet a few manuscripts of the original library still remained together—at least until the end of the nineteenth century—in the Grand Seraglio at Istanbul, after the drums and tramplings of four centuries.

The most famous of all libraries in ancient times was the collection at Alexandria. In the Western world it was the first large public library; it was the cradle of literary scholarship and of responsible publishing; it was part of the earliest university. In one form or another it seems to have lived for seven hundred years, although many doubtful legends have grown up around it, and its final destruction is wrapped in silence almost total.

The library, along with the Home of the Muses (or Museum), was founded by Ptolemy I, Alexander the Great's marshal and his successor as king of Egypt. Its administrators strove to have the best, the most authoritative, copies of all important books, collated and catalogued with utmost care. After two hundred and fifty years it was burned during Julius Caesar's difficult struggle to displace the twelfth

Ptolemy and set up his own mistress Cleopatra as monarch. Mark Antony, who succeeded Caesar both as the real ruler of Egypt and as Cleopatra's lover, gave her as a replacement two hundred thousand books from the rival library of Pergamum in Asia Minor; these were stored in the sanctuary of Serapis, and this new library survived until the Empire went Christian. (Tertullian says that the original manuscript of the Hebrew Scriptures translated into Greek, the Septuagint, was one of its treasures.) Then the pagan sanctuaries were turned into churches, and Christians and pagans fought a cultural and religious war in the streets. In A.D. 414 the Christian historian Orosius wrote that the stacks of the great library "were emptied by our own men in our own time." If anything survived for the Caliph Omar to condemn as fuel to heat the public baths in A.D. 640 (according to a late legend), it was only a group of departmental libraries.

The imperial library of Constantinople, in an even more turbulent city, had still more drastic adventures. Its founder, the Emperor Constantine, intended it to contain both Christian and pagan works and caused fine copies of rare books to be made on durable vellum. Revolt, civil strife, and invasion struck the library again and again, but it was constantly restored by the Greek passion for culture. A rebellion and a fire in the fifth century A.D. destroyed it, with over a hundred thousand books, including one monstrous object, a copy of Homer's two epics written in gold letters on a snake's gut one hundred twenty feet long. Three of the most famous Greek statues perished in the same blaze. Rebuilt, refilled, reopened, the library was closed again for almost a century during the religious conflict over the worship of images and holy pictures. It was burned and looted, at least in part, by the Fourth Crusaders in 1203–1204. Restored once again, it was still in existence when Constantinople fell to the Turks in 1453. The Archbishop of Kiev, an eyewitness of the invasion, said that more than 120,000 books were destroyed. And yet many precious manuscripts survived in private collections. Lost in the outbuildings or substructures of some old mosque, some deserted church or forgotten barracks, there still may lie, in sealed jars or dust-covered chests, priceless relics of the classical past, more precious than the Hebrew manuscripts found not long ago in the Genizah, or storeroom, of a synagogue near Cairo. One of our foundations, which find it so difficult to spend all their money, could make its name world-famous by financing a really successful document hunt in the chief cities of the former Turkish Empire.

The invading barbarians from the North, after many attacks, at last split the Greco-Roman world into two parts, an eastern and a western realm. In the west, those who were the heirs of the Roman Empire spoke Latin and tried to teach it to their conquerors. In the east, the language was Greek. For some centuries the civilized Mediterranean world had been bilingual by practice and by sympathy; but after A.D. 500 or so, nobody in the west could speak or write

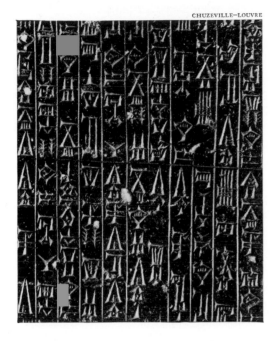

Many ancient kings have achieved immortality by committing their boasts and biographies to stone. Augustus's terse record of his achievements was carved, among other places, on a temple wall in what is now Ankara (above). The great Babylonian king Hammurabi (1728–1686 B.C.) insured the permanence of his famous law code by having it engraved on a diorite stele (left). A lesser monarch, Idri-mi of Alalakh (c. 1400 B.C.) is known to us only because he covered his own statue with his autobiography (right). The Persian Darius put an inscription on a gold plaque (below) in three languages: Old Persian, Babylonian, and Elamite.

79

Above are portions of three famous papyri discovered in inexhaustible Egypt. From the top, they are: Aristotle's Constitution of Athens, *copied in the 1st century and found in 1888; the speeches of Hyperides, found in 1847 and the first lost work of classical literature to be recovered in papyrus scrolls; and* The Tale of the Two Brothers, *the world's oldest fairy tale, written in Egyptian hieratic script in 1220 B.C. The Greek fragment at right, a label, bears the tantalizing words "Complete Pindar," but the book it accompanied was never found.*

Greek and nobody in the east could speak or write Latin. Now and then one still hears stories about Irish monks who alone were able to keep the knowledge of Greek alive in the west. Laudable, if true; but unfortunately false. An occasional scribe might copy out an occasional Greek word during the Dark Ages in the west, but the tradition of reading, understanding, and transmitting the Greek tongue—although it was the language in which the Gospels and the Acts and the Epistles were written—virtually died out (with the exception of a few lonely geniuses such as Grosseteste and Erigena) for a thousand years.

The second danger that confronted the Greek and Roman classics was not violent destruction but peaceful change. Nowadays it is almost impossible to purchase the piano works of Alexander Scriabin or to find scores of the music of Lully. Scriabin died in 1915; most of his music has been allowed to go out of print. Much of Lully still remains in manuscript, unpublished, unperformed, unknown. In the same way, those books which ceased to interest the Greek and Roman reading public ceased to be copied and studied, and were therefore not transmitted from one generation to another. After Vergil's *Aeneid* was issued, it was accepted at once as the great epic poem in the Latin language. It was learned at school, it was read for pleasure, it was admired and imitated. Naturally, it displaced all earlier epic poems, even the *Annals* of Vergil's greatest predecessor, Ennius. For a few generations, Ennius was respected, although little read. Then he was forgotten; his poem vanished. Nothing of it is left now, except fragments quoted by Roman scholars to illustrate oddities of archaic style—five hundred fifty lines in all, no fragment larger than a page. Only four poets of the early Roman Republic have survived entire, or almost entire: Lucretius, the philosophical missionary; Catullus, the brilliant lyricist; and the comic playwrights Plautus and Terence. All the others were neglected and eventually disappeared. No doubt some of them were trivial and others crude, but there were several masterful writers among them, such as the satirist Lucilius, and several lively works in minor genres, such as the Atellan farces, which we should dearly love to be able to read.

There was another habit of taste that tended to make books obsolete in the ancient world. This was sheer laziness. Partly to cater to lazy adult readers, and partly to create handy texts for use in schools, editors in later Greece and Rome reduced the complete works of many distinguished authors to small, neat anthologies, assimilable with little effort and easily portable. Thus, out of the eighty-odd plays by Aeschylus, the Seven Best were selected; out of more than a hundred by Sophocles, the Seven Best. These selections ousted the complete works, which fewer and fewer readers requested or even knew. So all the other plays of Aeschylus and Sophocles have vanished. With Euripides we are luckier because we also have part of one set of Complete Works.

If war is the supreme destroyer of books, it also, in another sense, creates them—as happened when the sack of Rome by Alaric and the Goths in A.D. 410 inspired Saint Augustine to write The City of God. *He conceived it as a reply to those who argued that the disaster, which in effect ended classical civilization, was a retribution for abolishing pagan worship. This French miniature was painted exactly a thousand years later, and shows Augustine offering his book to the pope even as the Goths are raging through the streets.*

81

Konstantin von Tischendorf

The page above is from what is probably one of the two oldest Bibles in the world, the fourth-century Codex Sinaiticus discovered by the German scholar Von Tischendorf on Mount Sinai in 1844 and brought by him to Russia fifteen years later. It is now in the British Museum, except for forty-three leaves in Leipzig and some fragments elsewhere. Its only rival for antiquity is the Codex Vaticanus of roughly the same date. Older than either, however, is the scrap of papyrus at left bearing part of verses 31–33 of the eighteenth chapter of the Gospel of Saint John. It was found in Egypt in 1920 by Bernard P. Grenfell and has since been dated to the first half of the second century A.D.—making it the earliest known fragment of any part of the New Testament.

Three thousand years after it was buried in the tomb of an Egyptian high priest, this papyrus Book of the Dead (a sort of guidebook to the next world) was unrolled in 1960 at the British Museum. It proved to be twenty-two feet long and, except for some wear at the beginning, in excellent condition.

Illustrated London News

But aside from these three, we have no Greek tragedies at all. Many of the lost books of Greece and Rome were not destroyed: they were allowed to slip into oblivion.

There were two further hazards that the classics had to survive before they could reach the age of printing. One was a change of format, the other was a change of script. The two changes sound unimportant, but they drastically altered our intellectual history.

Suppose that in 1970 all publishers decided to abandon publishing books in their present form and began to issue them only on microfilms; and suppose that we all accepted this, rearranging our homes around microfilm-readers and storage cabinets. If so, all the new books would be produced exclusively on microfilm. All important old books would be transferred to microfilm: the Bible, the encyclopedias, the scientific and technical manuals, the law books; and Shakespeare, Milton, Pope, Shelley, Keats . . . but who else? *

At once the question becomes difficult. Should Butler's *Hudibras* be microfilmed? and Langland's *Piers Plowman*, which nobody reads except specialists? and Cowley's epic on King David, which nobody reads at all? A selective grid has been created. Through it must pass any book in the English language that is to reach the postmicrofilm future. The rest will be kept in storage for a while, will be forgotten, and in a few generations will fall into dust. (We have in our own lifetime seen a similar series of changes in recorded music, from the old phonograph cylinders to the flat 78 rpm discs, then to LP discs; and now tape threatens to make all discs obsolete.)

Suppose also that we were to introduce a new phonetic alphabet, say in 1970: all our important books would have to be transliterated into the new simplifaid speling. Within a

---

* See "On the Horizon" (page 105 of this issue) and "Where Will the Books Go?" by John Rader Platt, in HORIZON for September, 1962.

---

couple of generations only a few experts and antiquarians would be able to read the older script. All the books that remained untranscribed would be neglected, difficult, remote. Soon they would sink into decay and oblivion.

Now, these two changes actually took place during the centuries after the Greek and Latin classics were composed and while they were being transmitted to us: the format and material of books changed, and then the scripts in which they were written.

In the flourishing days of Greece and Rome nearly all books were written on long narrow strips of papyrus, in parallel columns arranged from left to right. When not being read, the strip was rolled up around a central rod and (although its material was thinner and its dimensions generally smaller) looked rather like the "scrolls of the law" kept in Jewish synagogues today. Although brittle, papyrus is quite a good material for books: if it does not get damp, it will remain firm and legible for a long time. The dithyramb of Timotheus can be easily read today although it was written on papyrus three hundred years before the birth of Christ. However, the specially treated leather called parchment (named for Pergamum in western Asia Minor, where it was perfected about 170 B.C.) is far more durable. Since it has a finer, smoother surface than papyrus, it will take smaller and clearer letters. And furthermore, a book with separate pages sewn together at one edge is far easier to use than a long continuous strip which must be laboriously unrolled in order to find and read a single column of writing.

Therefore the Greeks and Romans gradually stopped using papyrus and gave up the roll format. (Actually, "volume," which comes from the same root as "revolve," means a roll. The word for the flat book with pages is "codex.") This change-over was not at first encouraged by governmental

TEXT CONTINUED ON PAGE 86

THE GREEKS
HAD A PICTURE
FOR IT

This stylish battle scene is proof that the lavish picture book is no recent invention, for it comes from what must have been an extremely handsome copy of the Iliad *produced—possibly in Constantinople—between the third and fifth centuries* A.D. *It is the earliest extant example of a Greek illustrated book, and in its original state it probably consisted of some 380 vellum leaves. Of these, only fifty-two separate fragments survive—and they only because a thirteenth-century collector who evidently preferred the pictures to the text cut some of them out and pasted paper over the backs. They came to rest in the Ambrosian library in Milan, where they were bound and catalogued merely as "a book of pictures." In 1819 Father Angelo Mai, the expert who discovered the Cicero palimpsest on page 77, peeled off the paper and recognized the text underneath as part of the* Iliad. *The inscriptions and captions had been added by later hands and were often inaccurate. This plate—which Mai numbered XXIX—shows the Greeks and Trojans in battle. At the left young Teukros is being congratulated on his successes by Agamemnon (wrongly identified as Diomedes), while overhead float the goddesses Athena, Hera, and Iris.*

διπροτειντιερσαν

ΠΡΟΛΟΦΥΓΑΓΟΔΑΚΗΥΧΕΟΝΤΑ
ΟΝΕΙΙΜΕΝΑΙΟΥΛΛΠΟΛΕΣΟΛΓ
ΕΤΕΛΕΙΟΤΑΤΟΝΠΓΕΓΕΗΝΩΝ
ΧΕССΙΤΕΚΟСΕΛΑΦΟΙΟΤΑΧΕΙΗС
ΠΕΡΙΚΑΛΛΑΞΙΚΑΒΒΑΛΕΝΕΒΡΟΝ
ΙΖΗΝΙΡΕΖΕΣΕСΚΟΝΑΧΛΙΟΙ
ΟΤΑΓΕΚΛΑΙΟСΗΛΑΥΟΕΝΟΓΝΙС
СΙΟΟΟΤΟΝΠΝΗΙСΑΝΤΟΛΕΧΑΤΙ
ΧΑΛΛΑΝΑΞΩΝΠΕΛΛΩΝΓΕΙ

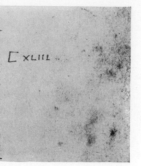

Since all books were copied by hand until the invention of printing, opportunities for error were limitless. At the left, underlined, is an example from the codex (i.e., flat book with pages) containing Trimalchio's Dinner *by the Roman satirist Petronius. The copyist, probably a monk, has written* abbas secreuit, *"the abbot isolated him"; but the phrase in the original was no doubt* ab asse creuit, *which means "he started with a nickel."*

TEXT CONTINUED FROM PAGE 83

authority and took quite a long time. But the Roman lawyers liked the codex shape because it was so easy to consult. The Christians, too, who wished to read parallel passages in the four different gospel narratives and to compare the prophecies of the Old Testament with their fulfillments in the New, preferred the large book which could be opened out flat; and scribes, both pagan and Christian, found that a parchment page would take graceful script and elaborate decoration far more readily than papyrus. The eminent British papyrologist C. H. Roberts suggests that the change in format was connected with the first written versions of the life of Jesus. Saint Mark, author of the earliest gospel, wrote it in Rome in the handy format of a parchment notebook with pages. This he took to Alexandria, and there (although they continued to use the cheap local material, papyrus), the early Christians grew accustomed to having their sacred writings in the form of a flat-paged book. By A.D. 400 the roll was obsolescent, whether in papyrus or in parchment. Any book that had not been recopied into the new format could survive only by exceptional good luck. And some Greek and Roman classics now lack their beginnings because the outside of the papyrus roll, with the first few columns of writing on it, had perished before it could be transcribed. Others are only part of a once larger set. Aristotle's *Poetics* was a two-volume work, one part dealing with tragedy and the other with comedy; but the second was lost before it reached the codex form and will now never be known—unless through a fortunate find.

All Greek and Roman books were, of course, written by hand. Great changes took place in Greek and Roman script between the fourth and the eighth centuries of the Christian era. In classical times the Greeks wrote most of their important books in what we call capital letters, without much punctuation and often with no spaces between words. (The Romans, after hesitating for some time, followed them.) But, after many experiments both in the Greek world of eastern Europe, Asia Minor, and Egypt, and in the Roman west, a radical change to a script more like our own was carried through: a script in which words are separated from one another and most of the letters are unemphatic, curved, and small (hence called "minuscule"), while only the emphatic letters beginning sentences, lines of verse, and proper names are capitals, or majuscules.

Then and thereafter all the books written like this, "ARMAVIRVMQVECANOTROIAEQVIPRIMVSABORIS," had to be copied in the new script, with its word divisions and emphatic capitals: *"Arma uirumque cano, Troiae qui primus ab oris. . . ."* * But the work of transcription from one form of writing to another was laborious and difficult. A scribe who was accustomed to reading and writing *"Italiam fato profugus Lauinaque uenit,"* sometimes made mistakes in reading and transcribing "ITALIAMFATOPROFVGVSLAVINAQVE-VENIT." Therefore when a scholar today sits down to edit a Greek or Roman book, one of his most important jobs is to reconstruct the various phases of copying and recopying through which it has been transmitted and to determine just what types of error were liable to be introduced at each transition. When a sentence in a Greek or Roman author looks doubtful or senseless, one of the first devices that scholars try is to write it out INTHEOLDVNDIVIDEDCAPITALS, and then see whether the misreading of one or two letters, or a failure to separate the words correctly, led to the error.

My favorite mistake of this kind is a matter of word separation. At the vulgar millionaire's dinner party in Petronius's *Satyrica*, the guests are discussing a friend who has just died. "Ah, he had a good life," they say, "the abbot isolated him, and he died a millionaire." There were no abbots in the days of Petronius, and anyhow the second clause is meaningless. In majuscules the phrase reads ABBASSECREVIT. Divide the words differently and drop one superfluous letter, and you get *ab asse creuit,* "he started with a nickel" (see above).

These particular ordeals—the transference of books from one type of script to another and from one format to another—were mechanical hazards to the survival of literature. There was another, far more destructive, which depended on

---

* The Romans had no sound in their language corresponding to our *v*. They used small *u* and capital *V* for both the vowel-sound *oo* (as in IVSTVS, iustus) and the consonant *w* (VIR, uir).

THE LAURENTIAN LIBRARY

Whether it was Boccaccio or someone else who saved the Tacitus-Apuleius codex from decay at Monte Cassino, the world has reason to be grateful. It found a home (beside an earlier codex, from Germany, containing the first six books of Tacitus's Annals*) in Florence's magnificent Laurentian library. Here the books were piled up on carved lecterns (left), with shelf lists at the ends, and secured by chains. Now there is only one to a desk and they are all protected by glass. At the right is a page from Apuleius's* Golden Ass—*a portion, in fact, of the charming story of Cupid and Psyche, which became famous in this version.*

theatre ceased to exist: for a thousand years men forgot the full power and meaning of drama, and the few plays that were permitted to survive were preserved mainly as models of fine Greek and Latin poetic and conversational style.

The pagan Greeks and Romans had also loved lyric poetry, which embodies or evokes song and the dance. Many of their lyric poems were loving glorifications of carnal experience: an invitation to drink ("the snow is deep outside and life is short") or rapturous desire for a beautiful body ("my eyes dazzle, a delicate flame runs through my limbs"). Others were hymns doing honor to pagan deities. Such poems were particularly hateful to devout Christians, so that the vast majority of them were allowed to perish. In Latin we have four books of songs by Horace and half a book by Catullus. In Greek almost all lyric poetry has vanished (or had vanished until the recent discoveries began): only Pindar survived, and only his Victory Odes. The rest disappeared, and even the Victory Odes came through the Dark Ages in one manuscript alone.

There was one curious way of survival for classical books, although it led through apparent destruction. For the sake of economy, scribes used to scrape or wash off the ink from pages on which a book had already been written and inscribe another book upon the cleaned surface. This could be done with papyrus, but it was both easier and more profitable with the tough surface of parchment. Usually it was a pagan book that was erased, and the Bible or a work of Christian divinity was written on the palimpsest, or cleaned-off, pages. But traces of the old writing would still remain legible underneath.

For instance: one of the best books by Cicero was his dialogue *On the State,* in which he discussed the rival claims of democracy, aristocracy, dictatorship (or monarchy), and a mixed constitution in which the powers should balance one another. He published it in 51 B.C. It was much admired and long read, but during the Dark Ages it vanished. Some medieval writers quote *On the State* as though they had actually handled a copy; but such citations are very shady evidence, for they might be secondhand or thirdhand. The great book hunters of the Renaissance were never able to discover a copy, although it was on their list of the Most Wanted Books.

However, in 1819, Angelo Mai, an expert in discovering old books beneath later books on a palimpsest surface, was appointed head of the Vatican library. There he discovered a commentary on the Psalms by Saint Augustine, which had been inscribed in the northern Italian monastery of Bobbio in the uncials of the late seventh century, over a manuscript of Cicero's *On the State* inscribed in the taller capitals of an earlier era (see page 77). Cicero's words could still be read and Father Mai published them in 1822. The book was incomplete, but at least a quarter of it was there. How many forgotten libraries still contain forgotten copies of forgotten works of doctrine, beneath which there sleep great classical masterpieces?

If you wish information to survive for many centuries, however, cut it on stone or bake it in clay; you can even paint it, if the surface is durable and protected from weather. Do not try casting it in metal, for someone will almost certainly melt it down.

The Emperor Augustus wrote his own autobiography, listing his chief honors, benefactions, and victories. It was deposited at the Home Hearth of Rome, with the Vestal Virgins, and a version in bronze was set upon his mausoleum in Rome. Both the original and the metal transcript have vanished. But a stone-carved copy was found in 1555 on the walls of a mosque in Ankara (see page 79); since then, two more copies, fragmentary but helpful, have turned up in southern Turkey. Only through these bits of stone do we know what one of the greatest rulers in history considered his greatest achievements.

Fifteen hundred years before him the king of a little state in what is now the Turkish frontier province of Hatay, after an adventurous and successful career, composed his own life story. His name was Idri-mi, and he was king of Alalakh in his time. He possessed less taste and less money than Augustus, so he had it carved upon his own statue—not even upon an epigraphic tablet, but over his actual face and his hard-earned regal robes (see page 79). Gazing out from eyes of black inlaid stone, his effigy sat enthroned in a temple for two centuries, speaking his adventures to those who could read. Then, in 1194 B.C., his kingdom was invaded by the northern barbarians called the Peoples of the Sea. His statue was wrenched from its throne and smashed into fragments. But after the invasion had passed over, a loyal courtier of the fallen monarchy crept back and salvaged the statue of the King, and buried it with respect. And there, underground, it was discovered by Leonard Woolley in 1939, and its long-silent boasts were read, and its eyes looked out again on a changed world with the same blank arrogance as before. His name and fame were forgotten; yet the stone that carried his message remained, with an immortality for which he could scarcely have hoped.

Two hundred years after Augustus, another public benefactor, on a smaller scale, went to a stonecutter with a document to be perpetuated. He was an elderly gentleman who lived in the small Greek-speaking city of Oenoanda in Lycia. Now it is a lonely heap of ruins in Turkey; then it was prosperous, civilized, but (the old gentleman thought) not quite happy enough. He was a devoted adherent of Epicurus. Epicureanism had taught him that the gods have no interest in this troublesome little earth; that terrifying phenomena such as illness and earthquakes and comets are all explicable, not through divine malevolence, but through nature; and that the duty of man on this planet is to cultivate his garden, keep quiet, and be happy. Old Diogenes, as he was called, had had a heart attack. He determined to use some of his remaining money and energy in showing his fellow citizens and their descendants the road to happiness. So he had a huge inscription cut and set up in the central square of his little city, explaining the chief tenets of the Epicurean doctrine. Now, all the voluminous works of Epicurus himself have perished; we have nothing from his own hand except three letters and some fragments and apophthegms. But the inscription set up by old Diogenes of Oenoanda, rediscovered by explorers and read by scholars in the nineteenth century, is one of the chief witnesses to an important philosophical creed that is not yet dead.

Laws and state announcements were often displayed on stone, for permanence and publicity. The earliest Greek legislation in existence is the code of Gortyn: it was incised on the curving stone wall of the odeum and still stands, perfectly legible, among the ruins of that city in central Crete. The names of Roman magistrates, some of them unrecorded in history books, appear on tablets of stone; so do the sums paid by the subject-allies of Athens to her imperial treasury; and so, too, the last effort of Roman bureaucratic government, the gigantic edict of Diocletian fixing the price of virtually every object of commerce throughout the Western world.

Records cut on stone or cast in metal were intended to survive as long as possible. Books passed from hand to hand and constantly recopied were deliberately kept alive. But there is a huge and steadily growing assemblage of documents that were, in the eyes of those who wrote them and used them, quite temporary. Many of them were actually thrown out as rubbish. Yet, by a combination of good luck and crazy chance, they have survived and become valuable. These are things written on ephemeral substances like papyrus and clay.

The records found in Mycenaean palaces (first in Crete) and deciphered by Michael Ventris in 1952, were apparently scratched on clay tablets that were not even fired: they became permanent only when the palaces were burned down.* Almost all of the papyri written in Greek or Roman lettering that we now have were found quite literally in rubbish dumps or in the ruins of abandoned houses. Since it scarcely ever rains in Egypt, they lay quite comfortably beneath the dry earth until modern searchers dug them up. The modern Egyptians thought it was about as stupid as digging in Western dumps for tin cans, but they co-operated, for a

* See "Homer's Age of Heroes," in Horizon for January, 1961.

THE
LIVELY REVIVAL
OF A CLASSIC

Ever since the recovery of Apuleius's Golden Ass *from oblivion (page 89) the romance of Cupid and Psyche has been a favorite theme of artists and writers—nowhere more than in France. A typical example is the painted ceiling in the seventeenth-century Hôtel de Sully in Paris (above). So is* Les Amours de Psyché et de Cupidon, *written by Jean de la Fontaine in 1669 and illustrated a century later by Nicolas René Jollain (left). Even more popular was Molière's* Psyché, *produced in 1671 with music by Lully, dancing, elaborate settings (below), and machines for wafting the various gods and goddesses to the heavens and back.*

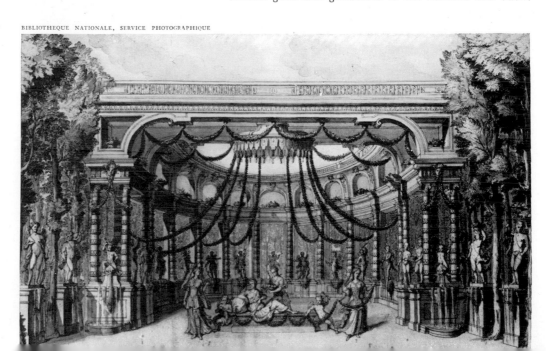

We would know a good deal more about the Mayan culture of Yucatán if Spanish priests and missionaries had not systematically destroyed the Mayan books. Only three survive. This is a page from one of them, known as the Codex Perez from the name written on its wrapper in a seventeenth-century Spanish hand. No one knows who Perez was, or how the book got to Europe, or why it ended up among some dusty papers in a basket in the Bibliothèque Nationale—where it was discovered in 1859. It is written on bark paper and is thought to be a ritualistic manual. Until a few months ago nobody could decipher the Mayan glyphs, but last March a group of Soviet scholars announced that by using electronic computers they had succeeded. Translations have not been published as yet.

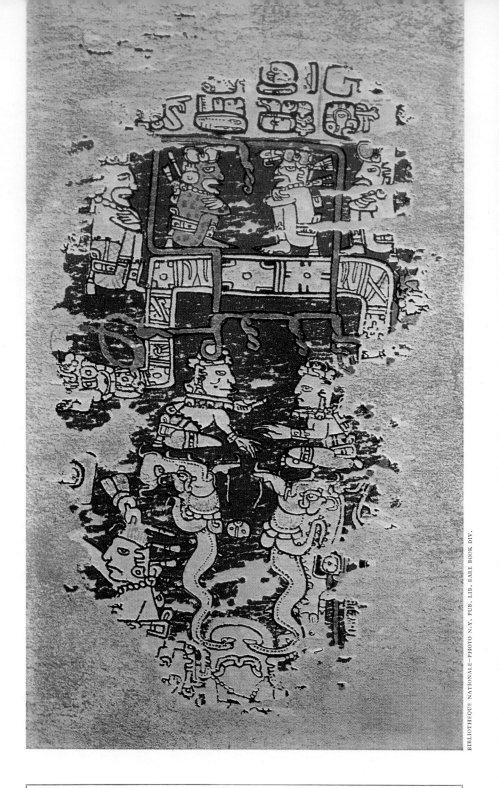

ON THE MOST-WANTED LIST

Gilbert Highet writes: Many hundreds of important Greek and Roman books have been lost that may yet be found moldering in a forgotten storeroom or buried in Egyptian sands. Every scholar will have his own list of longed-for works, but the following would most delight me:

1) The collected poems of Sappho

2) *Prometheus Unbound* and *Prometheus the Firebringer*, the two other tragedies in Aeschylus's trilogy (we already have *Prometheus Bound*)

3) Epicurus's masterwork, *On Nature*

4) The satires of the Roman republican "Whig" Lucilius

5) Livy's *History of Rome* complete (out of 142 books, only 35 survive; what we need most—hear me, Jupiter!—is his account of the civil wars that ended the Republic)

6) The emperor Claudius's *History of the Etruscans*

7) The autobiography of Hadrian

8) Porphyry's treatise *Against the Christians*

wage, and even imitated the excavators when they found how valuable the rubbish was. In one day's work at Oxyrhynchus (one hundred twenty miles south of Cairo) Bernard P. Grenfell and A. S. Hunt got thirty-six basketfuls of papyrus rolls out of one mound alone. These had apparently been discarded as worthless.

Some papyri have been preserved because they were deliberately buried. One of the oldest Greek literary manuscripts, containing the only known copy of a dithyrambic poem by Timotheus, was rescued in this way. It is an absurdly bad poem (although interesting to literary connoisseurs); however, someone prized it, for it was discovered in a leather pouch, laid carefully in the coffin of a dead Greek soldier buried in Egypt. And a truly magnificent copy of Book II of Homer's *Iliad*, now in the Bodleian library, was set in a coffin as a pillow beneath the head of a young woman, whose fine skull bones, small regular teeth, and black hair make us believe she was a beauty: certainly she was beloved. Other papyri—mainly letters, accounts, and official documents, though including a few treasures of literature—were found glued together or squeezed tight with water, to make cheap mummy cases molded to the shape of the corpse. (Out of one of these cases came part of the lost tragedy *Antiope*, by Euripides.) Even stranger were the finds at Tebtunis, where Grenfell and Hunt came on a cemetery of sacred crocodiles. One dead sacred crocodile is very like another, and the job of excavating these saurian mummies soon palled. Eventually a workman lost his temper and smashed one of them to pieces. Then it appeared that the crocodiles, too, were incased in molded papyri, and some even had rolls stuffed into their mouths "and other cavities." From such absurd hiding places do we recover the records of the past.

We have as yet no idea of the treasures that are hidden in the dry sands of Egypt and the neighboring countries. The oldest Latin papyrus ever found and the oldest text of Cicero (part of his most famous set of speeches), written down not long after his death, is now in Leipzig: it was bought from Egyptian dealers in the Fayum in 1926—and where did *they* get it? In 1945 a Gnostic library of thirteen volumes was found in Upper Egypt, containing, among other things, a Gospel in Coptic, adapted from a Christian work written in Greek, which evidently preserved some beautiful traditional words of Jesus. And an Oxford expert once told me, with affliction in his eyes, that among a pile of papyrus fragments he was classifying he had found a label (see page 80) bearing, in Greek, the simple words:

COMPLETE

PINDAR

In vain I besought him to go back to the collection and look through it again. "No," he said gloomily, "it isn't there. It must have been on the site in Egypt. But perhaps the excavator missed it when he was digging, or it had already been found and lost again, or someone stole it and sold it in Alexandria. It may turn up in twenty years. It may turn up tomorrow. It may be lying at the back of a drawer forgotten."

Last, most absurd, and yet most natural of all the hazards through which the classics had to pass was the barrier of human stupidity. When barbarism comes to outweigh culture, through foreign invasion or social revolution or deliberately nurtured sloth and ignorance, works of art are often taken to be "useless" and destroyed. In waves of materialism and in revolutions, everything old is apt to be judged obsolete. It is a barrier to progress; or it is lumber; or it is reactionary; or it is inedible and unspendable—away with it! Only last year the commissioner of antiquities in modern Greece, Spyridon Marinatos, told a sad story of the Second World War. A farmer in the western Peloponnesus was digging a well. Twenty feet down he came upon a stone box. He smashed in its lid. Inside there was a big object "like a bundle," dark in color and crumbly in texture. He thought he saw letters written on it. He informed the police, who informed the local director of antiquities; but for some time they could not get out to the farm. It was 1944–1945, and Communist squads were trying to control the roads. When at last the director was able to reach the farm, the object was gone. The farmer had thrown it on the dunghill "because it was not a treasure: it looked like dung and it fell to pieces quite soon." Others, however, had seen "many letters" on it and said that, although fragile, it held together on the dunghill for some days. Clearly it was a book roll: papyrus, or more probably parchment; clearly it was precious to the man who buried it in a stone casket; certainly it would have been precious to us. But it was of no use to the farmer, and it is gone.

And so it has always been. Boccaccio, who was a great booklover and book finder, once visited the monastery of Monte Cassino (see page 87). He was particularly eager to see the library, with all its treasures of handwritten books. Very humbly he asked one of the monks for admission to it. "Walk up," said the monk, "it's open." It was. It had no door; grass was growing on the window sills; the shelves, the benches, and the books themselves were shrouded in thick dust. Some of them, he found, had lost pages or even whole quires, others had their margins cut off. Boccaccio wept. He cried tears of pity "that the work and study of so many illustrious geniuses should have fallen into the hands of scoundrels." As he left, he asked a monk how such valuable books could have been so odiously mutilated. "Well," said the monk, "some of the brothers wanted to earn a few pennies: so they took a page and scraped off the writing and made little psalters to sell to children; and from the page margins they made gospels and breviaries and sold them to women."

When a bibliophile sees good books neglected and on the road to destruction, his first impulse is to rescue them. Say not "steal." " 'Convey' the wise it call," as Pistol says in *The Merry Wives*. Some splendid books from Monte Cassino are now in Florence. If it was not Boccaccio who "conveyed" them there, it was an even more fanatical booklover, Niccolò Niccoli; or an agent of his and of the house of Medici. One of these manuscripts alone—bless the hand that saved it— is the only surviving book that contains Tacitus's account of the civil war after Nero's suicide and of the reigns of Claudius and Nero; it also has Apuleius's wonderful romance *The Metamorphoses,* sometimes called *The Golden Ass* (see page 89). This magnificent codex, written in the eleventh century, now rests peacefully in the Laurentian library, above the cloister of the church of San Lorenzo. Near it is the only surviving manuscript of the first six books of another work by Tacitus, the *Annals,* found in Germany. Had these two manuscripts not been "conveyed," they might well have been cut up into amulets, and we should have lost one of the greatest historians who ever wrote of absolutism and the degeneracy of despotic power.

In 1844 a young Biblical scholar, Konstantin von Tischendorf, visited the remote monastery of Saint Catherine on Mount Sinai. There he found a great old book reduced almost to the same state as those which Boccaccio discovered in Cassino. It was a manuscript of the Bible, written in beautiful clear script between A.D. 330 and 400 and carefully corrected in or near that time. The book (see page 82) is now one of the chief treasures of the British Museum, which bought it from the Soviet Government in 1933 for a hundred thousand pounds. But when Tischendorf first saw it, nobody had paid any attention to it for seven hundred years. In the monastery, the latest intelligent markings on it, comments by readers, had been made in the twelfth century. Since then it had been brutally neglected. Fortunately, Tischendorf scented the value of this heap of waste. He copied out some of it and managed to get the monks to give him forty-three pages, which he took back to Europe and published. Fifteen years later he returned to the monastery, backed by funds from the Czar of Russia. This time he obtained the remainder of the poor battered Bible, which he carried away and published. In exchange, the monks received nine thousand Russian rubles. They were disappointed. They said that Tischendorf had promised to get them a steamboat.

Stupidity; censorship; changes in format and changes in taste; war; and of course the inevitable accidents, especially flood and fire—such are the hazards to the frail life of books. How did the great classics, Greek and Roman and Hebrew and others, ever survive them?

Ultimately, they were kept alive by men who loved books and knew that books are an essential element in civilization. The biography of one single book would fill many chapters. The British Museum owns a copy of the Gospels in Latin (see page 74), together with some writings of the early Christian Fathers, that has outlived storm and fire, sav-

agery and greed. A big book, over a foot high, with two hundred fifty-eight stout vellum pages, it was inscribed about A.D. 700 by Bishop Eadfrith in the monastery of Lindisfarne, now Holy Island, off the northern English coast. His successor, Bishop Æthelwald, bound it; and an anchorite living on the island made a jeweled case for it. In A.D. 875 the Danish pagans invaded England. The then bishop of Lindisfarne fled westward, carrying the sacred relics of Saint Cuthbert and this book. In a storm on the Irish Sea it was lost, but it was recovered at low tide as though by a miracle. For seven years it wandered; it survived more moves and invasions, and returned to its home at Lindisfarne, where it was catalogued (the simple boring work of librarians, which they think so unimportant and which is so valuable!). Next it survived the Reformation and the Protestant sack of monasteries, although it lost its jeweled case and its episcopal covers. Then, like many valuables during a revolution, it came into the possession of a government official (Robert Bowyer, Keeper of the Records in the Tower). From him it was acquired by someone who really knew what it meant: a genuine collector, Sir Robert Bruce Cotton. From him, because of a political dispute, it was confiscated by the Crown. It is now in the British Museum.

The most moving of all such stories, however, and most encouraging, would be the biography of an ancient book as a work of art and thought. First we should have to describe its author and the contemporary audience whom he meant to read or hear his work. Then, some time later, the Greek or Roman scholars who accepted it as a valuable achievement and edited it (as the work of Joyce and Eliot is being edited today); and then, as the Dark Ages set in, the far-sighted optimists (pagan like Symmachus or Christian like Cassiodorus) who preserved it from obliteration; and, after them, the monks who saved it once again by recopying it, to live on for many centuries; later we should meet the fine-scented book hounds like Petrarch and Boccaccio and Poggio and Aurispa who discovered it when it was forgotten and sometimes copied it out with their own hands; until finally, after more perils than a displaced person and more sufferings than a tormented prisoner, it emerged fifteen hundred or two thousand years or twenty-five hundred years after its birth, to be copied on a miraculous machine and multiplied through the work of scholars and publishers, and—incredibly—to reach an audience who loved it as dearly as those who were present at its distant birth. Even then the life of such a book is not over. It will be read by Shakespeare. It will inspire a picture by Rembrandt, a satirical parody by Pope, and a lyric by Keats. It will be edited by Housman, distorted by Picasso, translated into music by Ravel, and remain inexhaustibly vital, immortally versatile, today and tomorrow and into a long future, as long as there are a few men and women who can read, and understand, and appreciate true greatness.

Made in Italy for the fifteenth-century Hungarian king Matthias Corvinus, this copy of Ptolemy's Geography *(title page shown here) was carried off to Constantinople by the Turks in 1541, bought by the French government in 1778, and is now in Paris.*

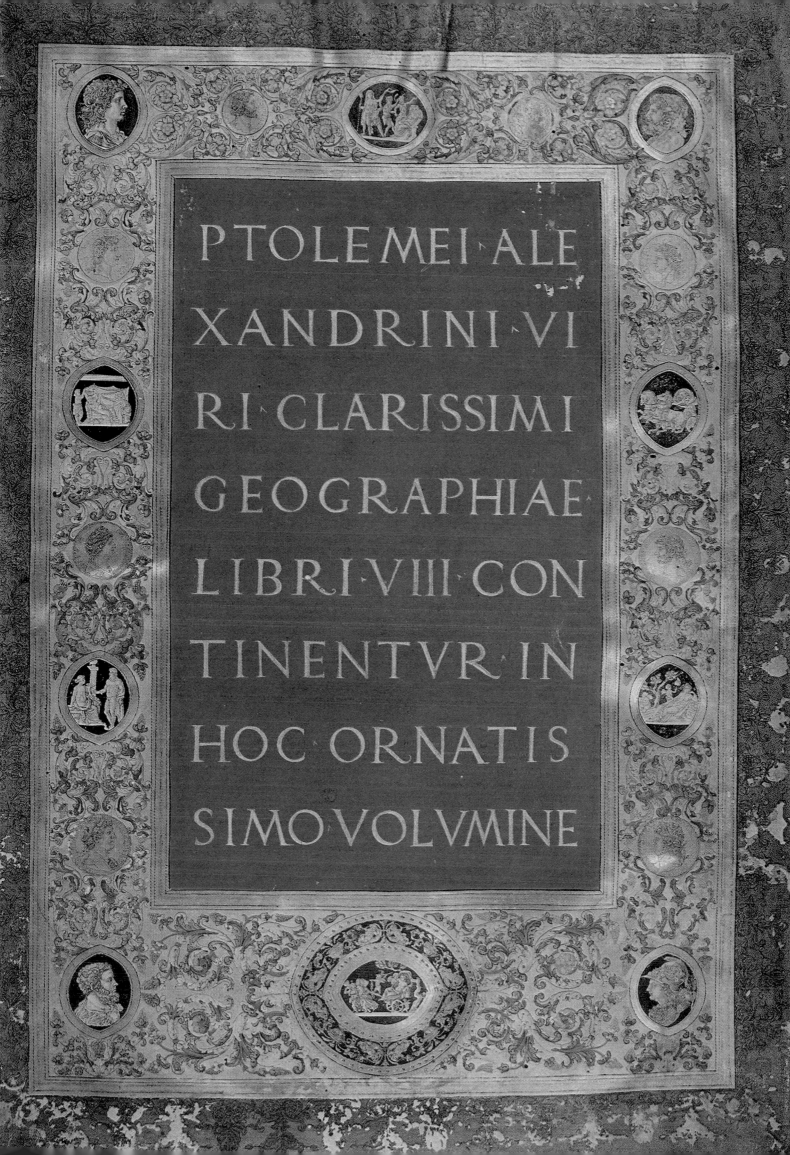

PTOLEMEI · ALE
XANDRINI · VI
RI · CLARISSIMI
GEOGRAPHIAE ·
LIBRI · VIII CON
TINENTVR · IN
HOC · ORNATIS
SIMO VOLVMINE

WHERE TALENT IS TRIED AND TESTED

TOM DALEY

By CHARLES L. MEE, JR.

Just how a small, off-beat, out-of-the-way movie house in New York's East Greenwich Village reflects anything about the whole "film scene" is not apparent at first glance. The Charles Movie Theatre serves a healthy diet of the old film classics, a spicing of "retrospectives" (such as the entire life's work of a given director), and an occasional special dish: for example, the work of Georges Méliès, the Frenchman who built the first motion-picture studio in the world and produced such memorable epics as *An Extraordinary Dislocation, A Trip to the Moon,* and *Monsieur Le Baron Has Eaten Too Much.* This is a good, if unorthodox, bill of fare, but it is not terribly unusual among the art movie houses. The unique activity at the Charles is its monthly Film-makers Festival.

Early last summer the Charles was about to close down. Its regular programs of "commercial" films were losing money. On June 28 it announced a week-long Film-makers Festival, something it had done before, but never for more than a day here and a day there. This time the idea caught on. The Festival was such a success that it was extended, and extended, and extended. Since then the Charles has gone on showing films of the established directors in what has come to be called the New American Cinema—Stan Vanderbeek, Stan Brakhage, Robert Breer, Richard Preston (Preston's spoof of the Kennedy-Nixon campaign, *The Candidates,* was especially well-received)—and occasionally some "classic" experimental films such as *Le Chien Andalou,* which was made in 1929 by Salvador Dali and Luis Buñuel.* But most of all, and this is what has made the Charles unique, it opened its doors to any film maker—whether neophyte or professional—who wanted to show his own work. Now, on the first Wednesday of every month, a strange assortment of film lovers arrives at the Charles at seven thirty in the evening. On such nights the price of admission is ninety-five cents or a can of film, and the program lasts far into the night—until the film brought by the customers has run out. This cinematic amateur's night has not only made the Charles solvent again but has provided the liveliest, most amusing and sometimes hysterical theatrical experience currently available in America.

The audience at these Festivals is surely one of the most tumultuous, demanding, critical, rambunctious, and appreciative ever to enter a theatre. It is made up of the people who brought the films—directors and their entourages, actors, scenarists, and producers—and others who have simply come to see what is new, what is adventurous, and what is "happening." It is an audience in constant turmoil: coming in, going out, standing up to jeer, calling out its most objective criticisms, spilling cups of coffee, filling the air with cigarette smoke, subsiding into reverent silence and erupting into ferocious applause, and occasionally getting into a scuffle in the aisles with an irate director whose film has just been hooted off the screen. It is an atmosphere of near-violent competitiveness, where the newest and youngest of all film makers are cutting their teeth—or sinking them into their critics.

There is a strong resemblance here to the "cutting" sessions where jazz musicians try to outdo one another, and in any Festival program there is bound to be a motley selection of films—some atrocious, some mediocre and, hopefully, some very good. But quality is not what makes them worth seeing. Artists learn by their own and others' mistakes, and at the Charles, because the audience is in no sense courteous, they learn quickly. It is the learning, and what one may perceive coming out of it, that is important. Here is a rare opportunity for young artists in a comparatively new medium to sharpen their talents and perceptions of one another through a thoroughly wide-open, knock-down-dragout forum. Since the beginning of the Festivals, hundreds of new film makers have been subjected to the rigorous test of pleasing an audience at the Charles Theatre.

If an artist's aim is to elicit a response from his audience, the Charles is the artist's dream; it is one of the very few theatres in the world where the possibility of riot is tangibly present. Whether greeted with insults or resounding ovations, the film maker who offers up his soul at the Charles can be certain of one thing: his offering will not be received with indifference and, whatever the reception, it will be instantaneous and palpable.

A typical recent program at the theatre was made up of fifteen films, each running from thirty seconds to thirty or forty minutes. (These are short experiments, rather than full-length feature films, some with sound tracks, some without, some simply "rushes" or unfinished "work prints" that will one day find their way into completed movies.) The first, bearing the appropriately melodramatic title *Out of the Night,* demonstrated why amateur film makers should be heard about but not seen.

It was the story of a man, with his own narration explaining what he was up to, who has decided to commit suicide. The viewer never sees him: his feet are shown, the top of his head, his hand holding a cigarette—and his gas oven. He explains that life is too much for him and goes to the kitchen and turns on the gas oven. Then he moseys around his apartment—better not light that cigarette—thinking, narrating, waiting. Finally, when he is so gassed (so to speak) that he can only crawl around the floor, he decides he wants to live. Suddenly life looks good to him again. Life

* See "Movies: Buñuel's Unsparing Vision" by Saul Bellow on page 110.

is worth it. He *wants* to live. He crawls out to the kitchen, reaches up and agonizingly turns off the gas—then flip-flops himself to the door onto his terrace, fresh air, life. After he revives he goes back to the kitchen and flicks on the top burner to make a cup of coffee, telling the audience how much he needs that coffee, how much he *wants* it (the simple pleasures); and the movie ends with a splendid, affirmative feeling.

There was a stunned silence at the end of this film (how could anyone in the *Village* do something so naïve?), and then one of those small, quiet voices from the rear of the house asked the fatal question: "How about that pilot light?" Another silence, and then a burst of applause; of course, if he could flick on the burner, there must have been a pilot light. Then, how can he . . .

One more director sent back to the old drawing board, the audience relaxed, apparently determined not to let any more inconsistencies slip by, and the Charles was off to a good evening. It is not easy to launch an attack on a movie as bad as *Out of the Night*, and somehow fruitless to waste time trying, but one small, nit-picking barb was precisely what was needed: a pin to prick the balloon and expend the audience's hostility toward a pretentious intrusion on the time they had set aside to savor and spend well.

The second film was a series of slides showing geometric abstractions in color. It received a murmur of appreciation; and then there was a film called *Motamotion*—some more abstractions, this time blobs and globs in motion. A pleasant but unexciting pair of films, and the audience seemed to stir, anxious to get things moving again. There was a peripheral argument between two directors, about nothing in particular, on one side of the theatre. A bearded beatnik spilled a cup of coffee on an intruder, someone from the upper East Side, while squeezing into his seat—an encounter more difficult for its social than its physical inconveniences. Proprietor Edwin Stein, host for the evening, stumbled over the reading of a poem written to go with one of the films, recouped, and managed to get the lines recited in what was presumably the correct order. And someone turned off the air conditioner to let the heat and cigarette smoke collect.

More films followed in rapid succession: an untitled work by Virginia Carteaux, a painter, was a striking piece of "action" painting in action. The first half simply showed (in black and white) splotches of paint being thrown onto a canvas and covered with more splotches, spots, globs, lines—the patterns constantly changing, repeating themselves, weaving into motion. It was something like seeing Jackson Pollock at work, developing a painting. The black-and-white film spun to an end, and the variations were repeated in vivid and, for the unliberated, embarrassingly sensuous colors.

There were three items in the program, aside from Miss Carteaux's contribution, that merit special notice. *Toys on*

a Field of Blue, by Gil Leveque and Richard Evans, was a persuasive antiwar testament. Far from aggressive, as so many antiwar plays and movies and demonstrators are (there must be a contradiction in *that*), the film showed a lighthearted, almost skipping old man who was on relief, suffering from shell shock received during the First World War. A few moments in his life were interwoven with another theme, that of two young boys playing, of course, at war. The two stories were developed independently, and only at the end were they brought together, ultimately, with a montage of the old man, quaking, worn out, destroyed by the war that had left him with nightmares, and the two boys, gazing with relish at their Christmas present—a large, toy guided-missile.

Early Bird, by Herbert Krosney, was a less ambitious undertaking, more in the nature of an experiment. It was not "experimental" in any sense, but represented a young director's groping with a simple story, testing the medium he wanted to work in. A man from Gramercy Park rises early one morning, goes out of his apartment building, and strolls down to the southern tip of Manhattan to have a look at the ships coming into the harbor. A bum begs a cigarette from him, offering a drink of his cheap whisky in return, and the two men set off to see a bit of lower Manhattan—the fish market, the first small trickle of people starting to work in the early morning. There is a delicate, fresh feeling to this film—perhaps because these early morning hours are among the few fresh, cool moments Manhattan enjoys. The bum and his distinguished companion then get into a taxi and go to Gramercy Park, presumably because in his flush of comradeship the gentleman wants to introduce his wife to the bum. When they arrive at the apartment building, somehow the one world of good fellowship dissolves into two worlds; the man presses a bill into the bum's hand, goes alone into the building, and the bum wanders on.

It is worth remarking that, although there was some dubbing of voices and sounds in the sound track of *Toys on a Field of Blue*, both these films relied primarily on visual images, backed with some unobtrusive music. The younger film makers—in contrast to the Hollywood directors who merely film plays—appear to have learned something from the silent films: that theirs is a medium primarily of visual images, not dialogue.

The third film that merits attention was *On the Sound*, a jazz-dance short featuring the dancers Mary Hinkson and Matt Turney.* The first film of Fred Baker, it was shot on Long Island Sound, in some pleasant woods and on the beach, and shows a young man meeting, dancing with, and finally disappearing into the woods with two girls.

Miss Carteaux's film, and *Toys, Early Bird*, and *On the Sound*, evoked warm, enthusiastic response from the audience; but there were some rushes from a "work in progress" that were received with catcalls and loud insults of a kind one rarely, if ever, hears in an American theatre. These

*See "On Stage: Matt Turney," pages 68–69.

"The director . . . retired from the scene of battle."

people are on the move, and they are impatient. If they see a bad film, they don't simply want it taken off the screen—they want it taken off, cut up, burned, and buried; and then they want the director drawn and quartered, tarred and feathered, and put out of the way once and for all so that he no longer takes up *anyone's* valuable time, or anyone's valuable movie projector, or anyone's valuable audience.

In any event, for this particular offering, there was such a stream of abuse, hoots, jeers, and guffaws that the director was not able to contain himself. Down the aisle he came: "Shut up! Why don't you shut up! Can't you people be a little courteous? These are goddam work prints. This isn't a finished film! Why can't you . . ." The director's language may have been stronger; the retorts were certainly outspoken, too, and their unfortunate recipient retired from the scene of battle holding what was unmistakably the short end of the stick. To describe the little scuffles that occurred, to say that a few people stomped out to the lobby to avoid seeing the rest of the rushes (arguing, shoving, shouting as they went) is perhaps unnecessary; but to do so does emphasize the fact that people at the Charles, whether directors or merely observers, reserve certain rights that most audiences do not—to express themselves however they wish, with enough forcefulness to have some effect.

What is significant about the Charles is not the verbal byplay, however, even though this is hard to beat for sheer entertainment. Nor is it any single film screened at the theatre. It is, rather, that the Charles lucidly demonstrates what is generally true of the young film makers today, European and American. They possess an aggressive candor, a sense of humor, convictions that are defended with heated integrity and, what is most important, a limitless vitality and excitability.

These are attributes not of people who merely produce movies but of artists. The Charles is a rare phenomenon because it encourages these qualities and so helps artists to grow. Whether the Charles presents a "typical" evening of newcomers like Virginia Carteaux, Herbert Krosney, and Fred Baker, or less ordinary fare that includes the big-time new American Cinéastes like Brakhage and Breer, Vanderbeek and Preston, this microcosmic underworld outpost of the cinematic artist illustrates—and illustrates so clearly because here it is stripped to the essentials—the new excitement that exists in the film world, the sort of excitement that makes Antonionis, Bergmans, Viscontis, and Truffauts. The Charles, and what it represents, is one reason why the old inferiority that film makers have felt with respect to the legitimate theatre is outmoded. In America the legitimate theatre might well feel inferior to the cinema. Certainly Broadway, when compared to the Charles, is a mortuary.

99

Newly found, this Marlik gold torso (four inches high) bears the crown, earrings, and posture of a king

THE ROYAL GOLD OF MARLIK TEPE

Beneath the mound of Marlik, in northern Iran, a king has guarded his treasure—and his secrets—for some three thousand years. From what was apparently a royal cemetery of a kingdom of the early first millennium B.C., the remains of a previously unknown people are now emerging. A rich gold trove of jewelry, cups, and vases in fine relief are being unearthed, along with highly stylized bronze and pottery animal figurines. The greatest surprise to scholars is the sophistication of these objects, found so far to the east of Azerbaijan, where before there was no reason to believe that, at that time, a culture of such distinction existed.

Marlik Tepe (see map, page 104) lies in the Gilan area of Iran between the great Elburz mountain range and the southern shore of the Caspian Sea. The mild climate and plentiful rainfall must have offered Marlik's earliest dwellers a land of rich and inviting fertility.

Who were the Marlik people? Were they natives to the land, or one of the successive waves of Aryans who began to sweep down from Russia as early as the third millennium B.C.? What kind of society did they live in? Starting with this last question, archaeologists have begun to reconstruct a picture of puzzling complexity. Cooking and milking pots, ladles, razors, and tweezers suggest a peaceful domestic scene, yet short swords and daggers, a bow and three thousand bronze arrowheads (some with double barbs) tell another story. Were the inhabitants warriors or merely farmers able to defend themselves against invaders?

Dr. Ezat O. Negahban, Technical Director of the Iranian Archaeological Service, and his team of young archaeologists hope to find answers to the riddle of Marlik during their current excavations on four neighboring mounds (one, called Pila-ghale, appears to be a fortress). Until now, the only writing that has come to light consists of a few characters on cylinder seals, so that a more definite dating of the Marlik culture rests on a comparison of the objects found with those of neighboring sites of the early first millennium B.C.

From a Marlik necklace hang pomegranates, an ancient fertility sign

Near the south shore of the Caspian,

three thousand years ago,

lived a skillful people whose recently

discovered remains startle

the eye and stir historical speculation

101

An unusual aspect of the Marlik mound is the fact that only one cultural level is found there. "The tombs were dug and fitted into the natural rock surface of the mound," writes Dr. Negahban, "and when the kingdom ceased to exist the site was never again occupied." Dr. Negahban reports from the site that four types of tombs have been found, and that in all of them the construction is fairly simple, in contrast to the extraordinary gold, bronze, and silver objects (some of which are shown on these pages) placed in them.

"The largest tombs are irregularly shaped chambers," as Dr. Negahban describes them, "about sixteen by nine feet, fitted into the natural rock, which was utilized for walls whenever possible. The gaps in the natural rock were filled with pebbles and clay mortar. From the type of articles found in them, they were apparently the tombs of kings or warrior chieftains. . . . These include equipment for daily use, for ceremonial and ritual use, for hunting and warfare, together with many decorative and documentary objects. The articles of pottery, bronze, silver, and gold show great beauty and fine craftsmanship."

The Marlik finds open up a realm of speculation. What contacts did these people have with their neighbors; what were the sources of the Marlik artistic motifs? The location of the Gilan area, northeast of Assyria, seems to have spared it at least temporarily from the onslaughts of Aramaean invaders from eastern Arabia, who reduced the powerful Assyrian kingdom to impotence and a "dark age" at the beginning of the first millennium B.C. When Assyria recovered, in the ninth century B.C., it engaged in constant struggles with the kingdom of Urartu, in the north (see overleaf), for control of the passes of the Zagros Mountains. Geographically in the center of the Assyria-Urartu contests lay the Mannaean village of Hasanlu, on the shores of Lake Urmia three hundred miles west of Marlik. In 1958 a remarkable gold bowl was discovered at Hasanlu, buried when the citadel was sacked and burned. Dr. Negahban believes—on the basis of objects that are comparable, and in a few cases identical—that the Hasanlu bowl was contemporary with Marlik.

The Marlik people seem not to have experienced these same invasions, but rather to have maintained a period of prosperity up to the time when, as Dr. Negahban puts it, "the kingdom ceased to exist." They developed a native art even where they borrowed current themes, though the question remains whether they were in direct contact with Assyria or merely sensitive to the fashions of the times.

"Cultural spheres have common, partly overlapping frontiers," writes Ernst Herzfeld in *Iran in the Ancient East;* "hence, shapes of things and decorations, techniques—though more deeply rooted in local conditions—ideas, and symbols may travel. It is not even necessary to assume direct or indirect trade." Dr. Negahban certainly concedes the contemporary motifs in the Marlik art objects. The winged bulls, griffins, and "tree of life" on the gold vase opposite

Bronze and pottery figurines from ancient Marlik resemble animals still found in the fertile Gilan region of Iran. The subject matter suggests an indigenous culture flourishing in the Marlik area as early as the first millennium B.C. A stag (top) of red pottery, his head turned to one side, has pierced ears and twisted horns, and stands almost a foot high. A bronze mountain goat (center) has human feet mounted on stands, while a humped cow (below) rests on wheels.

The griffins (top) and winged bulls (below) on this Marlik gold vase were common motifs in early western Asian art

are common themes in western Asian artifacts; for example on Nimrud reliefs or in the embroidery on the robe of Ashurnasirpal II, who reigned in Assyria from 884 to 859 B.C. (The winged bull would later appear on gateways of the royal palace of Persepolis.) However, Dr. Negahban also emphasizes the fact that Marlik was the product of a vital and original culture, which would have drawn its own inspiration from the indigenous plants and animals of the southern Caspian shore.

The pomegranate necklace (page 101) represents not only an ancient fertility symbol but a fruit native to Persia. Pliny considered it highly valuable, and the Greek physicians Galen and Dioscorides mention its medicinal qualities. Herodotus, too, says that when the Persians under Xerxes advanced on Greece in the beginning of the fifth century B.C., the King had a personal bodyguard of one thousand footmen who bore golden pomegranates on their spear shafts in place of the spike, and surrounded nine thousand others who bore silver pomegranates, virtually a Pomegranate Brigade. The humpbacked cow (a familiar figure on Mesopotamian cylinder seals), the stag and mountain goat (page 102), still exist in the Gilan area today, as do other Marlik finds (not shown here), a bear, a wild boar, and cranes.

The status that women occupied in Marlik society is suggested by a female figurine in bronze similar to a neolithic fertility goddess found at Hacilar in Anatolia.* During a similarly remote period woman's position was well established in Elam, the kingdom that prospered on the Iranian plateau from the first half of the third millennium B.C., where the royal line descended from the sons of the king's sister.

One puzzle, at least, is partially resolved by the Marlik discoveries, and that is the question of who might have been the forerunners of the Achaemenid goldsmiths. These artisans, who flourished during the Persian Empire founded by Cyrus in the middle of the sixth century B.C., must have learned their skills from just such traditions as would have been handed down from Marlik. Certainly the Marlik people, who are emerging today as magnificent craftsmen from a long-forgotten age, had the same creative energy which the Medes and the Persians were later to harness into the building of a great world empire.

* See "Man's First Revolution" by John Pfeiffer, in HORIZON for September, 1962.

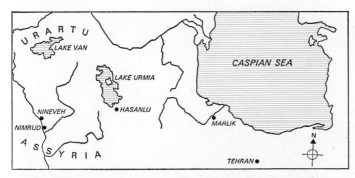

Marlik lay to the east of the Urartu-Assyria conflict

ON THE HORIZON

One of the marvels of human communication, as Gilbert Highet reminds us in "The Wondrous Survival of Records," (page 74) is that we can today hear "the voice, the very syllables and cadences, of a man who died some twenty three centuries ago." Dr. Highet's scholarly passion is that words and the books that hold them should be thus preserved, and he takes a dark view of the process—described with outright enthusiasm in the September HORIZON ("Where Will the Books Go?") by John Rader Platt—of reducing books to microfilm. In the past such transfers from an old technique to a new one, Dr. Highet suggests, have resulted in the loss of many texts. But does each advance in communication necessarily doom those that preceded it? What would happen, for example, if communication became total—if all the books were saved and the entire population of the planet could exchange words and images with one another.

We can assume that the technical problems will be solved. Even now it would be thoroughly feasible to subdivide the wave lengths of the air so minutely that we could have, say, a million AM broadcasting stations instead of several thousand. It is only a step of a few more magnitudes to imagine a world in which every human being could be assigned a wave length at birth, and be given at the age of discretion a little black box capable of sending and receiving the full range of audio and visual messages.

Every little black box would be in touch with every other little black box. Into it you would plug a wall screen, a hi-fi, and a facsimile reproducer for books and papers. From a central repository, at any hour of the day or night, you could dial up anything from Dr. Highet's favorite *Aeneid* to W. C. Fields in *The Bank Dick*. And you could broadcast, not only to your acquaintances, but to *everybody*. Theoretically there would be nothing to prevent you from going on the air and addressing all humanity.

But only theoretically, and that's the catch. For in order to address all of mankind you have got to let all of mankind know you are going to address them, and not by the same means you intend to use. You must first find some other way of getting their attention. From this follows a law, which will be known hereafter as the HORIZON Law of Non-Redundancy—namely, that all advances in communications recapitulate all other advances. In order for there to be TV, there must also be *TV Guide*. In order for there to be microbooks, there must first be books.

Survival is the prize we grant, and "classic" the name we give, to those almost miraculous works of the mind and imagination which still have the power to move us, even after twenty-three centuries. There will never be enough of them, as Dr. Highet's list of the great "lost" books makes clear, and the most extravagant technology will not make them any less necessary or valuable. For those who honor and live by books the future does not—in case you were worried about it—hold occupational unemployment.   E.L.

THEATRE

The Actors Studio Goes Legit

For the past fifteen years The Actors Studio has been the dominant school in the American theatre and possibly the most controversial organization in the theatrical world. Therefore the decision, made definite over the summer, to expand the Studio's activities to include a producing company is of more significance than the not uncommon announcement that still another theatre is in hopeful gestation. Two million dollars will be raised, a house in the Broadway area will be secured on a long lease, a large roster of actors (many of them Studio graduates) will be placed under contract for services as needed, plays will be optioned, directors will be assigned, and we shall see what we shall see.

Without quite knowing it, perhaps, we have been awaiting this sight for a long time. The Actors Studio has been a force without a face since its inception. Institutions with comparable authority in the theatre have almost invariably combined instruction with performance in an ascending curriculum—one graduates from class to stage. The most obvious example is the Moscow Art Theatre and its associated school, both under the direction of Constantin Stanislavsky, whose much-bandied Method provided the framework for instruction at the Studio and has given the name of Method actors to its alumni. Similarly, The School of the American Ballet is the nursery for the New York City Ballet, and influential schools are built into the Comédie Française, the Old Vic, and Sadler's Wells.

Lee Strasberg, who came into The Actors Studio a year after it was founded by Cheryl Crawford, Elia Kazan, and Robert Lewis, and who almost at once became its dominant personality, is a man of the professional theatre. As a youth he acted in Theatre Guild productions and was stage manager of the second *Garrick Gaieties.* But it was as a director of the Group Theatre in the 1930's that he made a permanent impression on the New York scene with productions of *The House of Connelly, Men in White, Gold Eagle Guy,* and *Johnny Johnson.* However, Strasberg has not worked in public for many years, and there has never been an acting company into which the students of the Studio could graduate. As a consequence, the procedures of this school have assumed some of the aura of a secret brotherhood, and the influence of the Method has been al-

most as widely suspected as it has been widely acknowledged. One hears that the Studio spoils actors in every sense of the word, and it is notorious that some of its more famous pupils display on occasion idiosyncrasies of headline proportions. One hears that Method actors resist direction, that they are preoccupied with the cultivation of their own emotional lives to the detriment of the emotions specified by the playwright and are given to quoting their revered teacher in disputes with directors under whom they are rehearsing. If all this is true, then Method manners must be infuriating.

Even more widespread is the notion that The Actors Studio propagates a mystique akin to some introspective religious experience. This view causes a New York *Times* writer, in a generally sympathetic article, to refer to Strasberg as the "resident guru"; it moves Paul Scofield, the elegantly disciplined star of *A Man for All Seasons,* to say in an interview published by *Show* magazine that, unlike the "Method people," he prefers technique to spontaneous emotion. "They have to be lucky to hit the bull's-eye without technique. What happens to them on an off night? . . . They have nothing to fill the vacuum with." Outside observers are not encouraged at Studio classes; the few who do penetrate come back with anecdotes about young performers being encouraged to "let themselves go" in spontaneous outbursts of intimate monodrama.

It all sounds unpleasantly visceral and professionally unpromising. It also sounds a little unlikely—unlikely, that is, that the Method is no more than a warm bath of psychological release. Lee Strasberg was working with Stanislavsky's directorial principles back in the days of the Group Theatre; in fact the Group introduced the celebrated Russian's ideas to the American stage—where, acknowledged or not, they have been influential ever since. The productions credited to the Group in the annals of the American stage—not only Strasberg's productions cited above, but the plays directed by Harold Clurman (Irwin Shaw's *The Gentle People,* Clifford Odets's *Awake and Sing* and *Golden Boy*)—were scrupulously disciplined and in some cases markedly poetic. Retrospective reports on the Group fall into the old trap of confusing the players with their parts: the 1930's nurtured the so-called theatre of protest in this country, and the plays written then were earthy and filled with social agitation. But the Group Theatre was not a proletarian workshop: on the contrary, it was an artistic utopia run by tough disciplinarians.

It is known that Strasberg has modified the Stanislavsky Method for use in America, but it is not plausible that, as the persistent rumors suggest, he has thrown away half of it. Stanislavsky, who was a gifted writer as well as an actor, director, and teacher of legendary prowess, conveyed his system to future generations in two now-classic books: *An Actor Prepares* and *Building a Character.* He had a highly organized, almost mathematical, mind, and he broke his curriculum down into a set of hierarchies as intricate as a royal family tree. The basic division was between the interior mental and emotional condition of the actor and the exterior communication of the play.

The first subject, discussed in *An Actor Prepares*, is an investigation into the ways by which an actor may find, within his own resources and experiences, intellectual and emotional correspondences to his stage role, and a description of the exercises that will enable him to evoke these states of mind and spirit in their original vividness for as many nights as the run continues. That is, few actors who are chosen to play Othello will in fact have strangled their brides, but almost every man and woman has suffered jealousy to some degree. Stanislavsky discovered that he could develop in himself, and train others to develop, a facility for recalling such experiences of pain or joy and adapting them to the given circumstances of the play. "Always and forever, when you are on the stage, you must play yourself." That famous sentence has caused much of the confusion about Method acting, it being supposed that Stanislavsky meant the stage to be a platform for enacted autobiography. But the "self" he had in mind is an imaginary being created from the "smelting furnace" of the actor's life and re-created in the role he is to play.

Building a Character, on the other hand, is a handbook of stage presence that begins with such fundamentals as walking and sitting (which must be relearned before they can be undertaken in front of an audience) and moves on to voice, placement, phrasing, and timing; the discovery of the play's essential theme (not to be confused with its overt plot); and the relating of characters to this unifying idea.

Thus Stanislavsky struck the balance between interior motivation and exterior craft that is implicit in every art. But, as Robert Lewis pointed out several years ago (in a series of professional lectures published under the title *Method—or Madness?*), the curriculum did not reach America in that balanced form: *An Actor Prepares* was published here in 1936; *Building a Character* did not appear until 1949. Students and practitioners of the theatre in America were thus for thirteen years in possession of a Stanislavsky system that seemed to concentrate on the state of an actor's soul and to concern itself not at all with how he should place his feet, move his arms, deliver his lines, or in general make himself the instrument of his playwright. Even the half of the system that was generally available was soon vulgarized by readers who reported, for example, that Stanislavsky held that to play a wanton one must be a wanton, and who overlooked in an eagerness for sensation his insistence on "as if" (Stanislavsky himself called it "the magic if") as the basis of the actor's imagination.

Strasberg and his Group colleagues had been to Moscow and seen at first hand the whole of Stanislavsky's curriculum. Nevertheless the Method acquired early in its career a reputation for psychological egocentricity, and

The Actors Studio has regularly been the butt of jokes and the victim of disparagement. How do we know, it is asked, whether Geraldine Page, Marlon Brando, Joanne Woodward, Paul Newman, Eli Wallach, Tom Ewell, and Ben Gazzara are accomplished actors because of what they have been taught in Strasberg's classes, or whether what Strasberg teaches has become solemn doctrine because, necessarily, a handful of the many aspiring actors who pass through his classes have been talented? In all honesty, the questions have been hard to answer in the absence of a theatre operating in accordance with the pedagogy.

*A*nother service the Studio Theatre can be expected to perform will be to focus attention once more on the performances actually taking place on our stages. In the lifetime of most contemporary playgoers, these stages have been dominated by texts. Anyone reading in the history of the theatre will discover that not so long ago the stage was ruled by its great performers—by Edwin Booth, Sarah Bernhardt, Mrs. Fiske, Duse, Macready, the Barrymores, to name at random a very few from a regal roster. We have stars—indeed our commercial theatre is hobbled by the star system—but for the most part these are monetary attractions, plums in the highly touted entertainment packages. Except for the Lunts (and they now appear seldom, and still less frequently in material of consequence), what actor today stamps his art on the theatre?

Reviewers seem to devote such acumen as they possess to discussions of the intellectual stature, ethical content, and entertainment quotient of the playwright's work. They make judgments, typically of a convenient generality, as to the "style" of a production. But when it comes to the work of the actors they resort to personal epithets—so and so was manly, such and such a miss was winning, a certain beldam was poignant. So, for that matter, are your postman and the girl who tots up your order at the supermarket. The darlings of the critics these days are for the most part these professional applause stimulators who conduct love affairs with the audience and leave their stage partners to the unproductive exercise of delivering their lines in a vacuum. Actors who play to the audience remind the audience of its own wit and charm; actors who play to the play draw the audience into a world of imagination, beauty, and virtue that the stage can offer with a vividness unrivaled in the arts. Stanislavsky said this almost every day of his life—it is at the heart of his Method.

In fairness, actors themselves are hardly responsible for the decline of their authority in the theatre. With the straitening of opportunity, with the increasingly hectic commerce of the theatre, they have become hired hands—and frequently not hired. One of the unceasing problems of the contemporary actor is that of finding a place to work—if not before an audience, then at least in a practice hall. Dancers must take classes every day, prize fighters avoid the gymnasium at their peril. The Actors Studio has been called a theatrical gym, and in that capacity it has preserved the techniques of many actors who might otherwise have been driven from the profession by the atrophy of their skill. Membership in the Studio is for life, and there are no fees: experienced players can be found there every day, sparring with one another to keep their hands in. Whatever arguments there may be about the efficacy of the Method, there are none in the profession about the value of the Studio as a gym.

Early in 1963, when the Studio Theatre opens, public attention will almost perforce be redirected to the art of live performance. I expect a period of wild and irresponsible comment as the critics and the audience grasp for standards of evaluation that have long been out of use. But discrimination will come with practice. There are no small parts, Stanislavsky once observed, only small actors. Now perhaps we shall see.

Ironically, the immediate motive for expanding the activities of the Studio into public production is not related to the craft considerations I have been discussing. It is being done because the Lincoln Center for the Performing Arts did not invite the Studio to become a part of its theatrical empire and Lee Strasberg was made angry by what he took as an obvious snub to the most influential stage school of the modern era. To make the wound even more painful, Elia Kazan has resigned from the Studio, pleading apprehension that his new directorial and administrative duties at Lincoln Center might produce a conflict of interest. It remains to be seen whether pique is a sound impulse for the Studio's new adventure.

Other aspects of the plans raise misgivings. In the first place, Strasberg is apparently unwilling to direct any of the Studio productions himself. His last foray into the theatre (*Peer Gynt* with the late John Garfield) was badly received, and he is reluctant to expose himself again. Instead, guest directors—a good many of whom have worked in the Studio's directors unit—will stage the plays.

The Actors Studio has always been ruled by committee. Stanislavsky ran his theatre and he ran his school; Balanchine is the master of his ballet company and of his school of ballet. Such control is not as democratic as committee government, but it may be closer to the nature of art. The recently reorganized directorate of the Studio consists of Strasberg, Miss Crawford, Geraldine Page, Rip Torn, and John Stuart Dudley. Under them will serve a production board consisting of Anne Bancroft, Frank Corsaro, Paul Newman, Arthur Penn, Fred Stewart, Michael Wager, and Edward Albee. In addition, Roger L. Stevens, the celebrated producer and real-estate operator, will act as general administrator (i.e., he will watch the money); and Max E. Youngstein, the president of Cinemiracle International, is being prominently mentioned as the man who will raise one half of the requisite two million dollars. This mixed

group of actors, directors, playwrights, administrators, and tycoons will have to serve with singular unanimity and selflessness if the project is not to founder on cross purposes and hurt feelings.

The plays known to be under consideration by the Studio Theatre are by Tennessee Williams, William Inge, and June Havoc. Miss Havoc's script is said to be autobiographical and that raises a flicker of interest, but the other names seem wrong for the venture. This is not said in disparagement of the writers: on the contrary, Messrs. Williams and Inge are discouraging in this context because they are so sure-fire. The responsible heads of The Actors Studio are all professionals and they naturally go about their business in a professional way; the danger is that they will achieve no more than a professional success.

Despite a lifetime fanatically dedicated to the theatre, Stanislavsky was never entirely professional, and perhaps the fanaticism was the proof of his amateur heart. Stanislavsky was, of course, a wealthy man (incredible though it may seem, he ran a lucrative family business on the side), and of course there was Chekhov. I will not ask that The Actors Studio Theatre find a Chekhov between now and January 1, but I would be more sanguine for its future if the playwrights it sponsored were not so little in need of sponsorship. (What can anyone do now for Inge or Williams? It is rather a question of what they can do for the Studio, and the relationship is uneasy.) And especially I would look forward to the new theatre with great expectation if Lee Strasberg would take responsibility for one of the scripts under contract and demonstrate in public what he has for so many years been teaching in private.

ROBERT HATCH

BOOKS

A Diary from the Depths

One of the best things about the literature of our time is that it is so various. A hundred years ago "modern books" were almost all English or French or German or American; they dealt almost entirely with aristocratic or middle-class life, and they appealed predominantly to upper-middle-class Western European standards. But now we read books originally written in languages that, a century ago, were closed to all but a few experts. Stories, letters, and autobiographies published in the last ten years take us to countries far away both in distance and in thought, and show us societies few of us could ever visit, far less penetrate. V. K. Narayan's novels (reinforced by such films as *The World of Apu*) give us some of that India which only Indians know; we hear the private conversation of a Japanese family in the Hataros' *Mother and Son;* and a goofy but entrancing West African talks to us in Amos Tutuola's *The Palm-Wine Drinkard.*

Brazil is a land hard for Americans to know. The language, though charming, is more out of our way than Spanish. Besides, Brazil is not one country. There are at least four distinct Brazils: the few big cities, the enormous inhuman jungle, the smaller towns and cities, and the arid, wretched Northeast. There is even a fifth: the Brazil of the Negroes, with its own religion blended from Christianity and voodoo, its own music, its own customs, and (at least in Bahia) its own cultural ties to the West African homeland. A Carioca friend of mine, white European by origin but long a naturalized Brazilian citizen, told me he had "naturally" never seen the Negroes of Brazil in their own society, "except at Carnival"; but, he went on, "you occasionally glimpse the black rooster's feathers and the bones and the ashes and so forth, in corners of the golf course, and often at night you hear the drums beating."

A special area of Brazilian life unknown to most Brazilians was revealed to them for the first time two or three years ago. A Negro woman, called by the beautiful name of Carolina Maria de Jesus, who had lived for twelve years in a slum of the great rich city of São Paulo, published an account of her daily life. Although her education had stopped very early, she had apparently composed much fiction and had tried without success to get it printed. Her diary, kept in old notebooks and revised with the help of a reporter named Audalio Dantas, was published first in a local newspaper and then in book form. A best seller in Brazil, it has now been translated by David St. Clair and issued in the United States by Dutton as *Child of the Dark.*

Is it genuine? Apparently it is. At least Carolina herself exists, she has been seen and interviewed, she has spoken to many audiences about life in the slums; and the diary reads as though it had really been written by a proud, bitter, ignorant, sensitive, starving, hard-worked, self-centered woman. From it (with the help of the translator's preface) we can re-create something of her history and the strange society in which she lived.

Carolina Maria de Jesus is forty-nine years old. The daughter of an unmarried field hand in central Brazil, she had two years' schooling, no more. At sixteen she ran away from home. About the first twenty years of her adult life we are told nothing, except that apparently she could not hold a job: when she was a servant, she

liked to slip out of the house at night and make love. She has borne three children: João to a Portuguese sailor (1947), José Carlos to a disappearing Spaniard (1950), and Vera Eunice to a Paulista businessman in 1953. (She actually gives his initials, and says he paid her a monthly allowance for the little girl.) It was when she was pregnant with the first son, João, that she sank into the depths. Jobless and friendless, she built a one-room shack out of debris in the *favela*, or shantytown, on the muddy banks of the river Tietê. And there she lived for the next twelve years, bringing up three children and supporting them mainly, if not entirely, by collecting and selling waste paper, tin cans, bottles, and other throwaways, sometimes by cooking and serving garbage. The children were nearly always hungry, and they had worms. The river was polluted: the women drew water from a single public spigot, standing in line, quarreling, and fouling the place.

Carolina says most of the men did not work, and there was a great deal of drinking, fighting, and fornicating. Such settlements exist all over the world on the outskirts of big cities: the cantowns (*bidonvilles*) of Algeria, the Bantu appendixes of Johannesburg, many more. A main point about them is that they are not urban slums, like the old Five Points in New York, or London's Whitechapel, or the Glasgow Gorbals, or the Alexanderplatz area in Berlin, which were all near the center of the city and were the poorest parts of real city life. The Brazilian *favelas* and other peripheral slums are apparently inhabited largely by country folk in exile, by peasants who have drifted in from remote fields and villages, and will not go back. Carolina Maria de Jesus herself was brought up on farms. Among her neighbors in the *favela* she mentions the Pernambucans, who sleep ten in a room; the Bahians, who "talk only with knives"; and the hard-working, frugal Northeasterners: all incomers, strangers to the lights, skyscrapers, and big business of São Paulo, and really living in a riverbank village, messy, primitive, and jolly.

The jolly, puerile, neolithic side of this life, with lots of singing and dancing and magic and dressing up in fantastic costumes, appeared recently in a delightful motion picture called *Black Orpheus*, which traveled between downtown Rio de Janeiro and its hilltop *favelas*. Carolina Maria de Jesus, however, tolerates none of that. She loathes living in shantytown, picking garbage for a living, trying to feed four hungry bellies, worrying about her children's morals (João, aged eleven, has been charged with rape), and defending her brood against the hostility of the neighbors. True, she may have had a gay life in earlier years, and she must still be attractive, because Senhor Manuel, a very respectable gentleman, has an affair with her, and there was a gypsy who, before he went north . . . The only sections in which her diary shows anything like tenderness (except when she writes of her children and her idyllic dreams) are short passages dealing with love proffered and accepted. Ever since she came to the slum, she has hated it. When she began writing, it was in the hope of selling her stories and escaping on the magic carpet of success. Yet the diary itself was apparently written with no thought of publication. It was like the record which a prisoner keeps, noting the injustices and debasements of his existence so that, by recording them, he may contemplate them in detachment and spiritually master them.

Child of the Dark is a sad book to read, but it is not easy to forget. Its style is simple, blunt, repetitive, but brisk and tasty. There are scraps of superstition in it, and slices of homemade poetry, and savory nubbins of political gossip. (Carolina believes that President Kubitschek sent Queen Elizabeth of Britain thirteen millions' worth of jewels as a birthday present, and she is bitterly opposed to the new aluminum currency because "money should be worth more than what it buys.") If the diary is genuine, it is a minor classic—because it is one of the very few books that have ever been written about the lowest and poorest, *les misérables,* by one of themselves.

In our knowledge of Greco-Roman society, one huge gap is that we have scarcely any records of the life of the slaves. A few gay allusions to flogging, fetters, and crucifixions in the comedies of Plautus and Terence, a few reminiscences in Petronius, a few character sketches and moral observations and epitaphs—these and some fantastic life histories and some appalling accounts of slave rebellions—from such fragments we must reconstruct the life of the submerged millions.

In modern times *The Road to Wigan Pier* and *Down and Out in Paris and London* are wonderful works, but George Orwell was a cultivated man, well read and widely traveled. The stories told to Dr. Oscar Lewis and edited from tape recordings and notes in his *Children of Sánchez* (Random House, 1962) deal with the life of the poor, yet come from a higher social scale than Carolina's diary: the father, Jesús Sánchez, has a regular job and supports three households. Maxim Gorky did live as a down-and-out, but his *Lower Depths*, once believed a shocking document of social realism, now seems romantic, rhetorical, and contrived.

Most of us look for three things in literature: eloquence, truth, and imagination. Carolina Maria de Jesus has only the primitive eloquence of the harried, hard-pressed mother with a family to feed; her imagination hardly goes further than the simplest symbols of popular art: princesses, jewels, stars, clouds. But her book contains an unusual proportion of that third ingredient, the seldom-told unpopular truth, which inspires in some compassion, in some revulsion, and in others revolution.

GILBERT HIGHET

MOVIES

Buñuel's Unsparing Vision

In recent months the Spanish-born director Luis Buñuel has startled movie-goers with the ferocious imagery of a film called *Viridiana.* This has been, commercially, Buñuel's most successful effort, though he has been making powerful films in France, Spain, America, and above all Mexico for more than thirty years—among them *Le Chien Andalou* (1929), *Land Without Bread* (1932), *The Young and the Damned (Los Olvidados,* 1951), *Robinson Crusoe* (1954), *The Roots* (1957), *Nazarin* (1959), *The Young One* (1960), *Stranger in the Room* (1961), and *The Exterminating Angel* (1962), the latter still unreleased in this country.

Buñuel—like Ingmar Bergman, Federico Fellini, and Michelangelo Antonioni—is one of the film directors whose views of the human condition must now be granted considerable importance. Movies have become more subtle than they once were; and the film director has joined the poet, the philosopher, the theologian, the scientist, and the historian to spin with them in the great vortex of explanations of our world. The film director enjoys a noticeable psychological advantage over the others. Because discussions of the human condition fatigue the mind and strain the will, we welcome views that can be assimilated in the darkness of the theatre by a relaxed and diverted consciousness. We may agree or disagree with stated opinions, but we rarely quarrel with images: these are immediately persuasive.

Thirty years ago the film was considered a vulgar art, or no art at all but a source of sensations for the masses. For the most part film directors were satisfied merely to make obvious, heavy references to the modern condition. In pictures like Chaplin's *City Lights* the comedy and pathos were primary and we were left to form our own conclusions about tender tramps and drunken millionaires. Chaplin's later films, however, are intellectually ambitious, his thinking becomes primary, and Monsieur Verdoux being led to execution says "Numbers sanctify." The state may slaughter men in quantities, but private enterprise in death leads to the gallows and the guillotine. The thought is not original; what is new is the appearance of a larger intellectual ambition in the movies.

Buñuel's work is certainly ambitious and intellectual; it is also truly impressive. He views himself as a sort of poet, and he is a radical and uncompromising thinker. Since *Le Chien Andalou,* the short surrealist picture he made with Salvador Dali in the late twenties, his social and religious concerns have been plainly visible. In a typical sequence from that film a lover whose face is strained with desire pursues a woman who understandably, even in surrealist fantasy, shrinks from him because he has a halter about his neck and is pulling a load that consists of two grand pianos, two dead donkeys, decomposing and slimy, and two priests in full clerical garb. These same elements—passion, terror, religion, death, bourgeois culture (the pianos)—are still present in Buñuel's latest work, though in richer, more mature form.

Buñuel's films have been shot in many countries and always deal with poverty. In almost all of them the starving, the crippled, the sick, the blind, the dead, are shown vividly and violently after the manner of *Lazarillo de Tormes* and of García de Quevedo and Pérez Galdós, Spanish masters who are famous for their hardness. Buñuel's *Land Without Bread,* which must be the most naked record of death by starvation ever made, was banned in Spain not, as I had imagined, by Franco but by the Republican government. Buñuel spares us nothing—nor himself, I must suppose—for there is nothing resembling sentimental manipulation in any of these films, no effort to exploit easy sympathies or to prick the heart and make it bleed a bit, a pleasant enough thing for the audience, in careful moderation. Unlike Fellini who, in *La Dolce Vita,* hovers over his horrors and often betrays an Italianate softness in the presence of blood and death, Buñuel strikes his blows in quick succession and does not linger over his effects.

Buñuel's views of Christianity have made him a controversial figure in Spain, of course, but also in France and in Catholic Germany and in the United States. Invited by the Franco government, in line with its policy of conciliating its famous exiles, to make a film in Spain, Buñuel made *Viridiana.* Too late the government learned it had been deceived. One version of *Viridiana* was confiscated, but the other got out, won a prize in Cannes, and was condemned by a Vatican critic for anticlericalism.

The beauty of this picture is miraculously inseparable from its horrors. The lovely Viridiana, about to take final vows, is sent away from her convent to pay a brief final visit to an uncle by marriage whom she scarcely knows. This uncle, an odd sort of recluse, lives on a neglected estate, plays Bach and Handel on the parlor organ, and with provincial Spanish innocence—soft-eyed, round-faced, touchingly unaware of his own perversity—dreams continually of the bride who died in his arms years ago, still in her wedding gown and veil. He occasionally wraps himself in her corset,

fondles her things, and when Viridiana appears, immediately recognizes her to be the image of the dead bride. She, during her brief visit, never for an instant relaxes her ascetic discipline; she rejects the bed to sleep on nails, cherishes her crown of thorns and, even sleepwalking, puts ashes in her bed. The eccentric Spanish gentleman, narcotized by his queer solitary life and his erotic devotion to the dead, is almost too remote from life to discern any wickedness in his desires. He does everything he can to prevent the return of the girl to the convent. He goes so far as to beg her to wear her dead aunt's wedding dress, as a very particular favor, and then, with the assistance of his housekeeper, he drugs her, and carries her sleeping to her bed. There he begins to unbutton the gown but cannot bring himself to take advantage of her. In the morning, desperate over her impending departure, he tells her she is no longer pure and cannot take her vows. Believing his lie, she leaves the house in horror, but she is stopped at the railway station by the police and brought back. Her uncle has hung himself with the jump rope of his housekeeper's little daughter. By the terms of the will, made just before his suicide, Viridiana inherits half her uncle's estate. The other half goes to his natural son, Jorge.

*P*enitent, Viridiana tries to expiate her sin of withholding forgiveness from her wretched uncle by filling the estate with as ugly a crew of paupers and beggars as she can gather, and to these nasty sinners she devotes herself with saintly piety; but we quickly understand, as does Viridiana's mother superior, that she is a proud, rebellious girl, a kind of Protestant who gives supreme authority to her own conscience. This second, Franciscan phase of her saintliness is shattered by the beggars and by her cousin Jorge. Jorge is a brisk, modern, masterful young man from the big city, who brings his mistress to the estate with him but is willing to ditch her for Viridiana (if he can get her), and for his housekeeper in either case. When the master leaves the estate briefly with Viridiana, the beggars get into the house and give themselves a banquet, which turns into an orgy of drunkenness, gorging, and copulation. They have themselves "photographed" in a travesty of *The Last Supper* by a gypsy who snaps the "camera" by lifting up her skirts. When Viridiana and Jorge return unexpectedly to the house, he is caught and bound while Viridiana barely escapes being raped by two of her poor, one of them a syphilitic. Her second venture into sainthood thus ended, Viridiana exchanges her piety for a sensual life with Jorge, whom she will have to share with the housekeeper. All three sit down to play cards to the loud banging of rock-and-roll music. This last scene suggests the room in Sartre's *Huis Clos* in which two women and a man are shut up in an eternal hell.

The transition from medieval Spanish Christianity to rock-and-roll requires about eighty minutes, but the thing is done with so much vigor and truthfulness, with such poetry and insight, that I do not think Buñuel can be accused of irresponsible brightness or muckraking or village atheism or shallow anticlericalism. The barrenness of the modern condition can give little satisfaction to so passionate an artist. Nothing is "exposed." Buñuel is not an admirer of tough operators. He remains, as he shows again in another recent movie, *Stranger in the Room,* an enemy of the bourgeois.

In *Stranger in the Room* a sleek industrialist with a little beard is first shown peeping into the clinic of his factory on a barren island where a worker is being treated for burns. What catches his eye, however, is not the unconscious victim, nor even the doctor, but a pretty little nurse whom he proceeds to pick up. The doctor's young bride is the spoiled daughter of a French businessman. She can't bear the suffering, "dull" poor and urges her husband to come back to Nice and lead a comfortable life. The industrialist fires and evicts a worker and is thus responsible for the death of the man's wife. The worker, crazed with grief, comes to the industrialist's house to kill him. There is a priest present who tries to reason with him, but what can a suffering worker have to do with the clergy, who eat dinner in the homes of the rich? He shoots the industrialist, and later commits suicide.

In this film, as in *Viridiana* and his earlier Mexican movie *Nazarin,* Buñuel applies himself to the same question: What is good in human life? Viridiana the would-be saint and the young priest in *Nazarin* apply their Christian measure to the realities of human nature and the facts of money and power. Violent truth sobers the priest; it sends Viridiana spinning into sensuality. The poor and the humble are not invariably good, but Buñuel rarely finds any virtue or even firmness of character among well-to-do people. Charity, courage, and friendship he discovers in the hard-pressed worker; in the peasant woman who offers a piece of fruit to a thirsty prisoner; in a girl capable of honorable love; or in the doctor of *Stranger in the Room* who serves the poor disinterestedly. But among those seeking sainthood or martyrdom in traditional form he sees only illusion; not sacrifice, but a perverse desire for pain; not love, but self-will.

It would probably be correct, however, to say that Buñuel is even more concerned with reality than with virtue and vice. Sin and goodness seem to him to have become irrelevant categories. But the wages of selfishness is perdition. If we cannot have religion, we can have reality, the acceptance of our true condition. But reality is social and collective, and Buñuel wishes to deal, as he himself says, "with the fundamental problems of today's man, taken not as a particular case, but in his relation to other men." In Buñuel's eyes reality is supreme, and

reality is authentically derived not from "particular cases" but from an entire society. The old story of the individual is exhausted, and was exhausted a century ago. Buñuel tells us: "Lack of work, insecurity in life, fear of war, social injustice, are things that, because they affect all men of today, also affect the spectator; but that Mr. X is not happy at home so, to amuse himself, he looks for a girl friend whom he will eventually leave to return to his wife, is undoubtedly moral and edifying, but leaves us completely indifferent." The comfortable man, self-concerned, attempting to embrace more comfort, bores us stiff. And what Buñuel is telling us is also what De Tocqueville forecast in *Democracy in America.* The scope of the individual has shrunk so that we can be interested only by looking at mankind as a whole. In the films of Buñuel the old self pursuing the old goals is unreal. The great question seems to me to be: When will we see new and higher forms of individuality, purged of old sicknesses and corrected by a deeper awareness of what all men have in common? Buñuel has not yet shown us what these forms might be. But neither, on the other hand, has anyone else.   SAUL BELLOW

CHANNELS

Abolish the Armchair Athlete

An academician of my acquaintance has reported to me upon developments relating to the institution with which he is associated. The academy in question happens to be a pocket billiards establishment, vulgarly known in times gone by as a poolroom, and my acquaintance is respected by all as a big man with the rack and chalk. His inside information was that shortly the ranks of All-Star Golf, All-Star Bridge, All-Star Baseball, All-Star Football, All-Star Bowling, and the like are to be joined on television by All-Star Pocket Billiards, featuring dour, sallow men in the act of banking the six-ball off the far rail.

As one high in the entrepreneurial ranks, poolwise, he looked upon this prospect with considerable pleasure. "It's bound to be good for business," he said. "Look what it's done for bowling!" His mind's eye was already bedazzled by visions of the immediate future: a sparkling salon, in which chandeliers have replaced the customary naked 100-watt bulbs, where gentlemen in dinner

jackets stop in for a bit of Kelly Pocket Billiards and ladies in evening gowns have become so hep that they need no longer be adjured to keep one foot on the floor.

I hastened to pass this news along to another acquaintance of mine, who in his own fashion qualifies as one of our era's most ardent sportsmen. He had come to me, one day last summer, with a mild complaint. The previous day had been a holiday, and he had passed it quietly at home. As I recall his account, he had settled himself before his television set at 10 A.M. to watch the New York Mets play a baseball game—or something very much like a baseball game—followed by the feature race at Aqueduct, a golf match on another channel, the first game of a double-header with the Yankees playing Los Angeles, the feature race at Santa Anita, and the end of the Yankee double-header. That concluded at 11 P.M., and "after that there was nothing at all," he complained. "Oh, I tried to watch professional wrestling for a while, but you know what that's like. Finally I just went to bed." He was aggrieved, with the air of a man who felt Hubbell Robinson was letting him down.

Obviously, he is a hard man to please. Saturdays and holidays are almost entirely given over to sports on television these days, and most of the hours between Church and Ed Sullivan on Sunday as well. As soon as Newton Minow made documentaries respectable by fiat, the Sunday intellectual ghetto vanished into weekday prime time and sports moved in. I suspect that sports now devours more television minutes than any other program classification.

It makes good sense. Television is at its supreme best when it can deal in real terms with real events, unpredictably unfolding before your very eyes. Even when a sports program is on tape, as most of them are, the outcome is unknown to the audience and there is the illusion of real tension and conflict. Watching a manned satellite being launched is even better, but it doesn't happen quite often enough to become a standard item. (Bearbaiting and feeding real Christians to real lions would probably be still more popular, but these are visionary thoughts and anyway where would you get real Christians any more?)

*W*hat I wonder about, however, is my academician's confidence that all this will be good for business. Pool on television may well mean more people talking about pool, but it does not necessarily follow that more people will be playing pool. I am not the only man who finds it hard, these days, to get together a foursome on Sunday afternoons: all the golfers are home admiring Jack Nicklaus and Arnold Palmer. The kids who used to rush home from school on warm spring afternoons to play baseball now rush home to watch it. And I have been in bridge clubs where all the tables were deserted and

the *aficionados* were in the TV room hanging on· Charlie Goren's every word.

Probably the easiest way to discourage the budding athlete is to expose him to the proficiencies of the expert. To watch Palmer hit a 280-yard drive, put a 2-iron on the green, and drop a 20-foot putt does not create any great urge to play golf. It might well create, in the average golfer, a profound urge to lie down and cry for a moment or two, but beyond that no thought of exercise is likely to intrude. At least, no thought of golf. Much of the satisfaction I get from golf comes on those rare occasions when I belt a ball 180 yards straight down the middle of the fairway—it happened once in May and again in September—and I intend to protect that sense of satisfaction even if it means kicking a hole in the television set. I am not even certain that a will as strong as mine will hold out forever. I begin to detect a mounting wish to sneak a look at Sam Snead once in a while. He hits them 290 yards.

Well, it's a trend, and I was never one to break my head beating it against a trend. If you can't beat 'em, join 'em, I always say; if you can't get a sawbuck, take a deuce. If television is to make spectators of us all, let us put it to good use.

Consider the population explosion, for example. Too many children are being born, and you can be sure we adults know how *that* comes about. Very well, then—all we need to do is make sex a spectator sport. It will take a little loosening of present laws, but they have been loosened quite a bit already, as anyone realizes who has seen Jayne Mansfield in a guest appearance. In this particular pastime, too, there are experts; let's round them up and put them on television, coast to coast. There should be no trouble getting sponsors. The perfume people, to judge from their current advertising, have been looking for something like this for years; and just today I saw a cosmetic product which informed the passing female that it contained "progenitin." That company is clearly ready for such a program proposition, whether it knows it or not.

After a while it will be just like baseball—everybody watching and no one playing. A little while longer, and the birth rate will topple.

It is a tempting thought and one which leads to a good many novel notions, all of them (in the present state of affairs) unprintable. I suspect, however, that those who are deeply concerned with the population explosion will continue to look toward other, less imaginative solutions, as they are constantly being exhorted to do. As for those who are deeply concerned about pocket billiards, they will have to look out for themselves. My own impression—derived, I hasten to add, exclusively from two viewings of *The Hustler*—is that they are quite capable of doing so.   STEPHEN WHITE

ROBERT R. MCELROY

What's happening? Answer: a "happening." What's a "happening"? Well, a "happening" is a new art form; it is an "event" that takes place in an "environment." This one is called *Ball,* by Robert Whitman, and it happened—if that is the exact word—at the Green Gallery in New York, where the "environment" was provided by colored paper on the floor and a paper canopy against the wall. In the "event," a large colored paper ball rolls on and off stage, two large paper lumps are beaten and doused with paint by four girls (see above), and in the final sequence—called "Falling Down"—the artist and a young lady fall down. Then they get up and fall down again. Then they get up again and fall down. And again, and again, and again. Finally—the end. Applause. Audience goes home. This is probably the origin of the expression, "having a ball." Question: Now we know what an art form is, all right, but who cleans up the gallery?

It was bound to happen sooner or later. The present Age of Abundance depends on waste, because if we don't throw things away we won't buy new ones, and if we don't . . . well, it's all in John Maynard Keynes somewhere, and you can look it up yourself if you're *that* interested. The point is that until recently no industrialist had the vision to realize the logical next step, which is to pay people to destroy his products. Now at last an automobile manufacturer, American Motors, has announced a plan to award dealers $50 for every trade-in

car they remove from the market or, to use less evasive language, junk (see below). We understand that the former president of American Motors, George Romney, is seeking public office. Will he be consistent and run on a platform of compulsory subsidized waste? We doubt it, and venture only the observation, for what comfort it gives Mr. Romney, that people like to act wasteful a lot more than they like to admit it.

UPI

I Hear America Singing

Addressing a meeting of the American Marketing Association at the Biltmore Hotel . . . William D. Tyler, executive vice president of Benton & Bowles, Inc., declared that advertising "reflects our society more accurately than anything else does. Esthetes and apologists can rail at its vulgarity, its brashness, its aggressiveness, its insistence, its lack of cultural values, its crass commercialism, its loudness and its singlemindedness—but let them rail," he contended. These are the qualities, "that have built the nation," Mr. Tyler said. . . .

Mr. Tyler is co-chairman of the Joint Committee for the Improvement of Advertising Content.

—from the New York Times

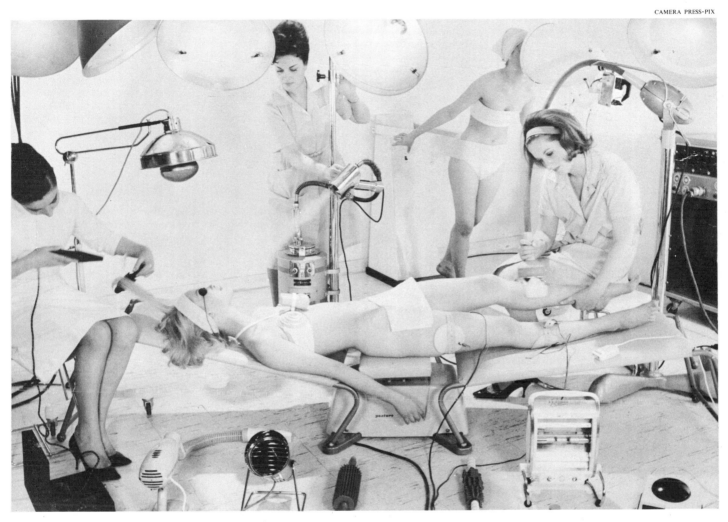

Mechanization takes command, even in the beauty salon. Feeling tired? Run down? Worn out by a facial and shampoo? Consider yourself better off than the model at center (above), who seems to have dreamt she was an astronaut in a vibro-massage bra. Baked, slaked, and shaken, she will presumably arise like some assembly-line Aphrodite, renewed in spirit if mildly mortified in the flesh. This nightmare of mechanical self-enhancement was put together to show the variety of "space-age" beauty equipment now available, but it almost seems better calculated to prove the French maxim: *il faut souffrir pour être belle.* Certainly the menacing array of instruments would discourage any but the most determined beauty-buff. Included are a vapor and heating machine, an ozone vapor spray, a hood and comb dryer, a belt stimulator, a spot reducer, two hand rollers, three different kinds of sun lamp, and six massage machines, among them a massage couch and a high-frequency massage comb. Sending satellites to Venus or aspiring to Venus-like charm, one is getting to be as complicated as the other. Over this photograph the London magazine the *Queen* put the simple heading: "All Systems Go."

Long Island Digs in for the Duration

The Francis T. Hunters have been giving a series of parties at "Blue Haven." None has created more comment than the dedication of the large air-raid shelter on the grounds, a below-the-surface replica of El Morocco. Many Hamptonians and their house guests came early and stayed on for dancing.

—from Hamptons Illustrated

115

Then

Now

What can have happened to Ekaterina Furtseva? Once there was a time when Khrushchev's good friend and colleague (at right, above, in 1957) exemplified what an American commentator unkindly called the "percheron" style in Russian femininity—stocky, severe suit, hair in bun, and all. Appointed Soviet Minister of Culture (opposite, at a Kremlin Film Festival), she emerged in low-cut lace, with trim figure and a new coiffure. "Our ambition," she has announced to the West, "is to become even more elegant than you." Now even a licensed electrician from Leningrad (opposite page, upper right) can blossom out in bare back and chiffon.

Signs of a "thaw" are much in evidence. Not only have the once-unsmiling delegates of the XXth Party Congress (below, left) become talkative at the XXIInd (below, right, with cosmonaut Major Gagarin), but reports out of Russia indicate a healthy preoccupation with such signs of modernity as bribery, juvenile delinquency, and the low quality of consumer goods. A decree of their Ministry of Finance has in fact advanced them years beyond us, by making it unnecessary to submit detailed *komandirovka,* which is Russian for "expense account." Where will it all end? HORIZON prefers to hope that we will be safe as long as the Russian for "dry cleaner" is *Amerikanka.*

Then

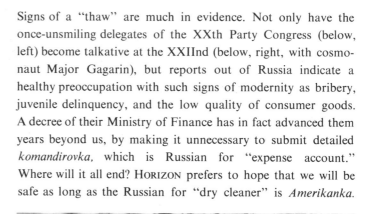

Now

SOVFOTO

CAMERA PRESS-PIX

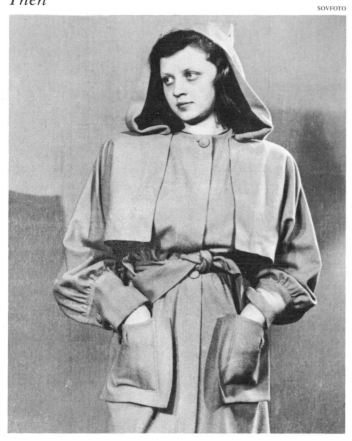

Patch pockets were all the rage in Russia in 1949, or so the Moscow Fashion House said—and who was going to argue?

Old-style Soviet kudos went to heroines of labor, like the muscular Khudovekov sisters of the steel mill at Magnitogorsk.

Improvement is shown by the fashion-show aplomb of 20-year-old Mila Romanskaya, who is identified as a genuine electrician.

Posing beside a pool in Rome, five Russian swimming stars can stand as symbols of a less arduous, and less grimy, era.

SOVFOTO

UPI

LONG FORM, SHORT SHRIFT

By JOHN KEATS

*W*e, the People, insist that if you wish to make music, or listen to it, you must pay a tax for this privilege. If you choose to waste your time at the theatre, at the race track, or watching grown boys play games, you must first help the rest of us to purchase our necessary hydrogen bombs. No one questions your right to worship as you please, but if you would follow Scripture, and take a little wine for your stomach's sake, you owe a tax to our secular democracy. If your child wishes a bit of sugar on his bread, you must pay a tax on that sugar, unless you are a cow. If your house catches fire, and you want us to help you, your frantic telephone call to the fire department is wisely taxed. If you would exercise your undoubted right to travel freely among the several states, you must pay a tax on your tickets, unless you are dead. In America only a corpse, or a corporate employee, is entitled to a tax-free ride.

Cynics have seized upon the last point to suggest that our Congress is the chorus from *Oedipus,* chanting "Count no man fortunate who is not dead," but theirs is a sniveling complaint. Such folk cannot or will not see that our Federal tax laws are not a jumble but, in fact, hew to a single line. All of our taxes are specifically designed to restrain any excesses of the human spirit that may unfortunately arise from too indiscriminate an individual search for life, liberty, and the pursuit of happiness.

In essence our tax codes are sumptuary laws, designed to distinguish between the necessary and the frivolous, as well as to minimize the possibility that a man might fall into the sins of pride, covetousness, and envy. Thirty years ago we expressed this in the phrase "Soak the rich." Today, however, there is widespread grumbling in the land, simply because so many of us have become rich enough to pay the taxes we originally sought to impose upon the few. Therefore, lest a public clamor grow to amend or otherwise vitiate our wise laws, it behooves us to recall how intelligent, and just, they are.

Our Federal income taxes, for instance, are predicated on the obvious truth that money has a marginal utility; that the more of it you have, the less it means to you. The high rates charged the rich are in no sense confiscatory but, like mercy, bless both him that gives and we that take. For the rich man, denuded of the greater part of his income, cannot but feel that he has helped us all, while we, in turn, are filled with a sense of tender compassion for one we have dragged down to a level approximating our own. There can be no quibble here that a progressive scale of taxation violates the Constitutional provision that taxation shall be uniform, for without charging the rich a pro-

gressively higher rate, how else could our singular uniformity—and our consequent sense of spiritual well-being —be achieved?

In order further to strengthen the national character, and to insure against any tendency on the part of the individual to prideful lusts, we have imposed a Federal excise tax upon all that is unnecessary, such as electric light bulbs.

Who really *needs* light bulbs, so long as the sun also rises? It is no more than natural to rise with the sun, and to go to bed with it, and any man who would hold back the night has set himself against God's Plan. Therefore, light bulbs are a vicious luxury, quite properly subject to tax— unless they burn in a factory or place of business. In that case their cost may be considered a tax-deductible business expense.

The test of our sumptuary laws is always practical social utility, and for this reason excise duties are levied upon the sale or communication of all that is of merely aesthetic or cultural value. We therefore tax the sale of musical instruments but not of dandruff removers, providing that the dandruff remover promises only to remove dandruff. If, however, the dandruff remover also promises to enhance your appearance, then it *is* subject to an excise tax, for while your dandruff is a social menace, your personal appearance is no concern of ours unless you selfishly seek to improve it.

The same stern test is made with respect to religious matters. Wherefore, we do not tax you if the cross about your throat be made of unglazed clay, but we will not permit you to go tax-free if yours is a cross of gold. Only our warriors are allowed to wear tax-free jewelry. True, we make them buy their golden badges of office out of their allowances, in order to teach them that rank hath its responsibilities, but we exempt them from our sumptuary law in token of our respect for Caesar. With that single exception, however, we tax all personal adornment, arguing that it can serve only inutile, personal ends. (You can, however, improve the appearance of your place of business and claim a tax deduction for the cost of this practical, socially necessary expense.)

*O*f course, we tax all products designed to waste time, such as athletic and recreational equipment—fishing rods, for instance—that can be used only by single contestants. But we wisely exempt athletic equipment required for participation in team sports, on grounds that a nation of football players is more virile and purposeful than a creekful of fly casters. Thus we decry all idle games that tend to glorify the individual but subsidize those sports that teach the virtues of grit, pluck, and self-abnegation. Indeed, when we think of the individual, we demand that he be so rugged as to live in a state of nature. Therefore we insist, through our taxes, on the Spartan home. Air conditioners, gas, electric, and oil appliances, television sets, matches, radios, refrigerators, phonographs, records, motion-picture projectors, flatirons, fans, kitchen equipment, doorbells, and garbage disposers—all of them time-wasters or life-softeners—come under sumptuary taxes. For we know it is possible to burn or bury garbage. You can rub two sticks to start a fire. You can bundle under blankets by night, and by day your useful exertions for the common good should keep you warm enough, so that an oil furnace is an uncalled-for luxury. There is no reason why you cannot bang on a door for admittance, rather than ring a bell. Anyone can press his pants between two boards under the mattress, so irons are hardly necessary. Anyone can carry his belongings wrapped in an old shirt, suspended from the end of a stick, and thus we tax luggage of all descriptions, including leather wallets. Or, if an old shirt will not do, anyone can carry his personal goods in motorcycle saddle-bags slung over his shoulder, since motorcycle saddlebags are properly exempt from the excise tax, for reasons that escape me at the moment but which no doubt are very good reasons. In sum, an American family that would escape our income and excise taxes would seem necessarily to live in an unheated log cabin on a homestead tract that provided bare subsistence; the family's males clad in football pads and its females in hockey jumpers, none of them traveling except by shanks' mare, and all of them innocent of the sound of Stravinsky and the taste of sugar, tobacco, and strong liquors.

But our laws permit, nay, encourage, the existence of another sort of American family to whom father's salary is merely a fringe benefit. They are my neighbors; I know them well.

Through a series of judicious exemptions to our taxes, we permit my neighbor to maintain, tax-free, three yachts and an island in Canada as a necessary business expense. He does not own these properties; his corporation does. If none of his corporate colleagues has ever set foot upon either the yachts or the island, this is because my neighbor is, after all, the president of the concern and hence is in the best position to determine the wisest use of this company property. Claiming those exemptions so prudently held out to businesses, my neighbor allows his corporation to send him periodically about the world by various means of first-class accommodation; to send him to the theatre with those persons who conceivably might someday buy something or other from his corporation; to install him in a mansion that not he but the corporation owns; to be brought into the city each day at eleven in a corporate limousine reserved, with its salaried chauffeur, for his use.

Nor is our dispensation limited to the corporate president. His satraps also enjoy luxurious entertainment, accommodation, and transportation without personally paying the taxes due on these consumptions. Further, untaxed funds from corporate earnings may be set aside for all employees in the form of pension plans. No such privilege is currently extended to the self-employed individual. We believe that if a man wishes to set himself up as a private lawyer, doctor, artist, writer, or actor, he must pay us a tax on any income he selfishly wishes to set aside against his old age. Likewise, if a doctor or lawyer wishes to raise his son in the profession, he cannot deduct the cost of his son's necessary education from taxable income, although the cost of educating a corporate employee can be written off by the corporation. Similarly, a writer (to use a miserable example) cannot easily claim an exemption for the cost of his third-class passage to France to conduct research among museums for his wretched historical novel, although the cost of the corporate research and development necessary to an improvement of girdles, for instance, is clearly in the public interest and is therefore tax-exempt.

*F*urther, the self-employed man can never claim himself as a business asset, even though he is the only asset he has. Thus, while income from an oil well is substantially exempt from taxation on grounds that the well will one day run dry, no man who lives by his wits is allowed to depreciate his brain, even if each passing year increasingly confirms it to be a swiftly depleting natural resource. There is no inconsistency here, for the purpose of our laws is to encourage Americans to join our great corporate ventures as an act of patriotism, in order that we may outrace the Russians to the moon.

The matter is simple: it will take money to reach the moon. We can acquire it only through taxation. Almost any corporation earns more taxable income and produces and consumes more taxable goods than any individual could. Thus corporations are more efficient tax collectors than a disorganized rout of relatively impecunious individuals. Corporations first estimate the taxes they will owe each year and add these to the price of the products they intend to sell, and the revenue is turned over to our Government at the point of sale, to the great benefit of us all.

Thus we will insure that our populace is happy while remaining morally pure, and that our nation's business is smoothly done by a process of each corporation's taking in every other corporation's washing, as it were, with the burden of taxation uniformly falling on everyone and on no one, as the authors of the Constitution surely intended. Best of all, no one will have been individually responsible.

John Keats is the author of several works of lively social criticism, among them The Crack in the Picture Window *(suburbs) and* The Insolent Chariots *(automobiles).*

MITOSIS BY MARTIN

A cartoonist looks at cellular subdivision

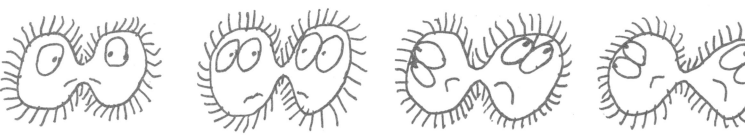
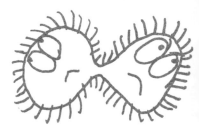

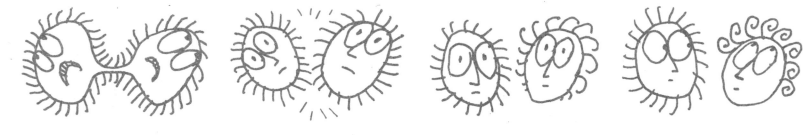

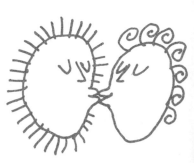

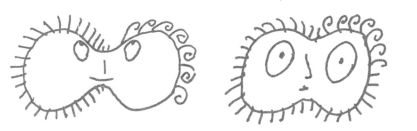

JEROME MARTIN